ON EARTH AS IT IS...

Gladys S. Lewis

BROADMAN PRESS
Nashville, Tennessee

To that Homer of my seventeenth summer
and to all those since
in whose cathedral shade
I have learned
how heaven
must be
in the swing of altars
through the will of God
in the daily things
on earth as it is

© Copyright 1983 • Broadman Press
All rights reserved
4263-32

ISBN: 0-8054-6332-1
Dewey Decimal Classification: 266.023
Subject Heading: MISSIONS, FOREIGN // MISSIONARIES
Library of Congress Catalog Card Number: 83-70006

Printed in the United States of America

Prologue:
In a Call to Missions

In July of my seventeenth summer, I became a Christian. Through the ups and downs of adolescence, my "rebellion" was into the church.

I wanted to take the step long before I did, but felt a reluctance to do so because of self-knowledge and always being 150 percent into whatever I do. I knew the decision would be rather incidental after the initial establishment in the kingdom. Certain the steps that would follow would take me far from any plan of my own at that time, my hesitation was neither from fear nor a shrinking from public commitment. I just wanted to be sure I would be willing to complete what I started, wherever it took me.

And I was right.

Six months after my conversion I responded to a compulsive, possessing inner drive to spend my life somewhere doing something unique to myself to share the amount of revelation of God I had with other people. Actually, that call, as we title the possession, was with me from conversion. I just needed six months to get the semantics right to express to people what I was doing.

Since I was in nursing school at the time, the call found definition as a career commitment to medical missions.

I established contact with the Foreign Mission Board and with firm resolve started through the requirements for appointment as a foreign missionary.

A year and a half later I met a first-year medical student who had come to my church to give a devotional in the young people's Sunday School department. He had been a missions volunteer since he was eight years old. That wasn't the first attraction he held for me, but it seemed somewhat providential once I got around to thinking about it. I had felt from the first that our names went together—Wilbur and Gladys. The sound of those names together made me think of pet goats.

Well, goats need love too. We found love in each other.

But, lands, was he slow!

My nursing school was Catholic and as long as I was locked up in the nunnery, he was as complacent as a preacher with a 100 percent return of signed tithe cards. But once I finished my nursing education and went to Oklahoma Baptist University for my bachelor's work on a campus seething with young ministers, my Lochinvar swung into action.

Between semesters of his senior year, we were married in the church where we had met four years earlier.

In the next six years we finished degrees, internship, residency training in surgery, and military service; birthed a daughter and a son; were appointed medical missionaries assigned to the Baptist Hospital in Asunción, Paraguay; and studied a year at Southwestern Baptist Theological Seminary in Fort Worth, Texas, and a year at the Spanish Language School in San Jose, Costa Rica.

Finally, with our babies and with all our worldly goods in eighteen barrels and three crates, we chugged up the Paraguay River on a riverboat, en route to our destiny. We were strangers in a strange land, but warm and confident in the companionship of the One who called and sent us.

There we were, trailing clouds of glory, to save all of Paraguay. To my surprise, crowds of Paraguayans did not meet the boat and fall down on their knees, begging me to tell them about Jesus. As a matter of fact, no one met us. There had been a mix-up in schedule because the river level was down. We were not expected to arrive when we did! The river was so low that we had to transboard in mid-river to a flat barge to get on to port where we were put out on a mud bank instead of the wharf which was twenty feet above our heads. When we found out the Spanish word for barge is *chata*, which is the same word for bedpan, we thought it symbolic and fitting that we began our missionary career by putt-putting onto a mud bank in a *chata*.

A good thing had happened to me back in the days of my seventeenth summer in my new birth postnatal period. I had six weeks of the only free time I had had before or have had since. I had quit my high school summer job to get ready to enter nursing school. Lovely, empty hours stretched about me in every direction. Three structures held me that month and a half. Two were spiritual: Bible study and prayer. The other was kind of spiritual too.

Some sylvan identification has touched the inner recesses of my being. I love trees. No. That is not all of it. I am lifted and transported by trees. There is some empathic symbiosis between the image of growth and stability in the stalwart green tree and my transient, but eternal spirit.

The particular tree that touches the poet in my soul is the cottonwood. At the alley edge in my seventeenth summer backyard was a Cadillac of a cottonwood. I called it Homer because of my odyssey there.

Every afternoon of that delicious empty space in my history I settled myself in Homer's cathedral shade to learn about the Bible and prayer. While the leaves twisted in the slow summer air or whispered to me with the stronger gusts, I read the Bible. From the midday hot, blue sky until twilight purple, I read. A gate pass to Eden was granted to me by my three structures; Bible study, prayer, and Homer.

I learned quickly, then slower and deeper with Bible study and formed habits that sustained me then and continue to do so now. Prayer was something else. I knew it was communication with God. But what was it? How could I do it? What did it do? I prayed every way I could think of to pray and about everything I could muster to mind. I tried every posture, attitude, and method that anyone would suggest, and a few no one has suggested yet!

Somewhere toward the end of that furlough in paradise, I found a verse that told me to pray without ceasing. That compounded my dilemma. How could I pray and never stop? That didn't make sense.

Then I read that I was to have the mind of Christ. Next I discovered that the evidence of having the mind of Christ is the fruit of the Spirit: joy, love, peace, longsuffering, gentleness, goodness, faith, meekness, and temperance. Those evidences of the mind of Christ would be found in the commitment expression of the believer, I was told.

If the mind of God is present with and in my mind through his indwelling Spirit in my heart and life because of my faith in Jesus as my Redeemer, then prayer—or communication with God—which is unceasing is a practice of openmindedness with God as I take in every experience, thought, and occurrence of daily existence.

My responsibilities in this relationship through the years have centered in my sphere, *my* world on this earth as it is, moment by moment. I filter life through this open sharing. It is not a conscious, labored thing. I have lived with the Spirit so long that I know he is there inside, like I know my heart is beating, and he knows he is not shut out of any of my mind and heart, whether the processes are intellectual, emotional, or spiritual. He is with me in a difficult book, a pique of anger, a new person to meet, or problem to solve, as well as with a plea for a sick friend, an agonizing burden, a hush of worship, or the joy of a long-awaited victory.

Prayer is an opening of myself to God to channel and funnel and filter what is going on with me at any time. I know that the Father is with me and hears me, but I never presume on him. By faith, expecting his interaction, I just offer what is going on and share my thought processes.

Persistence in prayer needs has come to my attention enough that I keep at it, but I keep in mind that God is Creator and Father and I do not feel the need to pester or harangue him. I am a parent. If my children ask me for something, I give it to them if I can and if it is for their good. I grant God greater respect and intelligence for me as his child than I assume to myself for my children.

But I do like the fellowship with him of shared experience of life as I go about on my earth as it is. He trusts me with my creative abilities to make my mark for him on my earth as it is. He intervenes as I need him, but he works usually at the front end of the processes by being in my mind to help with the initial judgments and reactions.

That's how I pray without ceasing.

Prayer is my communion and commitment of what is in me with God on earth as it is.

And I'm pretty busy on earth as it is.

I leave heaven to him.

Contents

The Model Prayer

Father,
You always are,
And in Heaven.
May your name be revered,
Your Kingdom established,
And your will be done
ON EARTH AS IT IS,
And even also is done in Heaven.
We ask for Bread day by day.
Please, do forgive our debts
Just as we have forgiven them who owe us.
You do not lead us into temptation.
Deliver us when we are in the tempting places, led
    by ourselves or others, and please, do,
    keep us from evil.
    (Paraphrase of Matt. 6:9-13
    by Gladys S. Lewis)

1
In the History
of the Host Country

Malignant heat from the January Paraguayan sun makes the house a giant sauna. I sit in my living room and shift my weight evenly and periodically so the sweat outlines on my clothes will not be concentrated when I stand. Spread before me are several wooden carvings of local models of *Guarani* Indians.

Senora Ibarra says, "My husband and I heard you are having an anniversary. He say to me, 'You go to the Baptist Hospital and give to the *senora* of Dr. Lewis our *felicidades* ("our congratulations").' And I say to him, 'I will do that, and I will take her some of this new work of yours. She may want to buy a gift to take to her mother when she goes to her country.' You will be glad to see your family, no?"

"That will be a while yet." I smile at her.

"But *los misioneros* are your countrymen, your family here?"

"They are. We feel a great love from our Paraguayan friends too."

"As do we. But home is still home."

I look from the carvings to Mrs. Ibarra's face. She is small, bird-like. Even her voice has a staccato quality, softened by the *th* sound on the *d* in Spanish, which is evidence of her direct issuance from Mother Spain. Her pointed chin follows a line drawn by her fine nose. Intense attention from jet eyes gives the effect of two spots which balance lines between upper and lower face.

"You've been here longer than we," I say.

"*Si*. We came in search of a new beginning after our Civil War and World War II."

"Your husband's work is well known."

"Carving was not his first art in the beginning. But no one wanted a furniture sculptor here any more than in *Espana*."

"I'll buy these Indian heads."

"*Muy bonitas* ('very pretty')." She separates them from the other things on my coffee table. Leaning toward me, her voice is low. "My husband say to tell you that he have time from his *conpromisos* in two weeks to make for you *la mujer*."

I remember the lovely head of a market woman that Mr. Ibarra carved for an exposition at the American Embassy. A protest forms. "I don't think I can afford . . ."

She interrupts. "The price to the American army man is not your price."

"But . . ."

"My husband knows you love his work. That pleasures him and pays part of his fee."

"I'll have to talk . . ."

"No talk. You come in two weeks. He say you and he make changes in the sketch so you have an original."

"*Senora* . . ."

"He say you come when he has the clay head made to be sure it is like the sketch. He has one request."

"What is that?"

"You have a car. He wants you to drive him to the river where the best cedar wood is."

I stand, laughing, shaking my head, and go to the study where the daily cash waits on duty to be spent. Counting the price of the head plaques into her hand, I say, "You are *amable* ('very nice')."

"I tell him you come in two weeks!"

Going with her to the gate, I wait as she walks from the house on the dusty road past the church on the compound and through another gate to the street. Turning, I retrace my steps on the driveway. The grape arbor provides some barrier from the blazing sky, but I feel the heat of the cement through the soles of my sandals. As I open the front door I think of the Ibarras and other

European refugees we know who fled to South America after World War II to start a new life. I walk down the hall to the study where the wooden shutters are closed against the heat, sink into a chair, and lock my hands behind my head. I stare at the ceiling and think of all the immigrants who have shared this heat with me.

The first great wave of immigrants were the military, the conquistadores, from Spain who came in the 1500s, bringing Spanish culture, religion, and colonialism. They were looking for gold, en route to the silver of Peru, but found the wealth of Paraguay as they marched and plied up rivers through central South America. Paraguay's riches lay in natural beauty and peaceful, agrarian Indians, the *Guarani*. The Spaniards left a contingent of men at a lovely, natural harbor formed by the Paraguay River on its way to join the Paraná system that flows by Buenos Aires, Argentina, and Montevideo, Uruguay, before emptying into the Atlantic.

The settlement and fort were founded August 15, 1537, and named *Nuestra Senora de la Asuncion* ("Our Lady of the Ascension"). It has remained in continuous existence but bears the shorter name, Asuncion, now. The Spaniards killed or enslaved the *Guarani* men and married the women—sometimes. A breed of people arose that had the inborn rigor and endurance of the conquistadores and the gentle charm of the *Guarani*.

Priests accompanied the soldiers, intending to save indigenous souls. But the priests' presence usually resulted in the softening of the spirit for secular exploitation. Men of the cloth were welcomed in the conquest, for their tireless efforts to civilize the pagans made the soldiers' job easier. Missionary orders of priests were formed to meet the challenge of the lost new world. The greatest, the Society of Jesus, was founded in Rome in 1539 by Ignatius of Loyola. Within twelve years, Jesuits were in Brazil. In a short time their influence spread over huge areas of the Paraguay-Paraná River systems.

A *Guarani* uprising in the early 1560s alarmed the Paraná region. When three Jesuits showed up in Asuncion in 1588, they were welcomed as God's helpers; the Jesuit era in Paraguay began. Jesuits built communities, called reductions, for the Indians.

I wipe the sweat from the back of my neck, close my eyes, and mind-measure the size of the ruins of the Jesuit reductions near Encarnacion, in the south of the country. I recall topless columned walkways, a roofless church, and a prison filled with dirt and wasps. Staring angels on facades with sightless eyes give rise to reverie as to what they might have witnessed.

The reductions were like cities where Indians were gathered to live in communal groupings on rigid, regulating schedules to be educated and Christianized. The settlements were self-sufficient in food and industry to supply their own needs, even to the point of raising armies for self-defense and to maintain their tie to Spain.

In spite of conflict with the colonists and Portuguese slave raiders, the reductions prospered. By the end of 1600, 100,000 people lived in the mission empire of the reductions. In the mid 1700s, the Jesuits as a society had become so wealthy and powerful that the crown became suspicious of their loyalty. In 1767 Charles III expelled all Jesuits from Spanish lands and ended with a pen stroke an empire within an empire. Some of the Indians clung to the reduction life; but by the early 1800s, the system had disintegrated.

The dog scratching at the back door reminds me to feed her. In the kitchen I pour myself a glass of iced tea and move about in an attempt to create some movement of air. I return to the fan in the study to read until the sun is down and it is cool enough to do some work.

I flip on the fan by the typing table and the small Paraguayan flag used by the children in the independence pageant at school begins to flutter. I sink back into the chair with a book but watch the blowing flag.

Paraguay became a republic in 1811 at a time when other

Spanish colonies were also claiming independence. The first head of the republic was Dr. Francia, *El Supremo*. His austerities, atrocities, despotism, and beneficences are truth, fabrication, and legend. He sealed Paraguayan borders and created a land that was a dominant force in South America before his death in 1840.

Upon the ascendance of Carlos Antonio Lopez, Paraguay enjoyed cultural, economic, and political leadership in South America for twenty-two years.

Lopez sent his oldest son, Francisco Solano, a military protégé, to Europe in an effort to make Paraguay known. The diplomatic party left in June 1853 and returned in January 1855. An ardent Francophile, Solano astounded Napoleon III in Paris by putting French troops through a drill. He absorbed French attitudes and social customs and took on an ambitious Irish mistress, Eliza Lynch, who left her Russian paramour in Paris to return to Paraguay with Lopez.

While Solano built a war machine and prepared for his dreams of expansion and empire, *La Madama,* Eliza Lynch, rebuilt Asuncion, architecturally and socially, with the French artists, intellectuals, and architects she imported. Her residence was on the site occupied by El Gran Hotel and her theater survived the decades of destruction.

"I'm on my way to the afternoon clinics," Wilbur says from the door. "You look amused."

"I was thinking of Justice Anderson and Madame Lynch's theater."

Justice, church historian from the seminary in Buenos Aires, had come to Asuncion with his wife, Mary Ann, for Wilbur to deliver their baby, Susie. With my enthusiasm for Paraguayan history, I spent several days showing Justice around and helping him get the baby's birth registered.

We pulled up in the garden of the Gran Hotel at noon. The euphoria I felt from having as an audience one who shared my enchantment with the past paled a bit. I knew he wanted to see the place, but he was reserved.

"Maybe you'd better go ask if it's all right for us to look."

"Sure, it's OK!"

"You talk to them first."

"I bring visitors down here all the time."

"After you check, I'll come in."

"The manager lets me go in the door that went backstage!"

"Should you introduce me to him?"

"They don't care when I come to look."

"Maybe I could look in the window." This was not the exuberant historian who had walked about the old Recoleta with its church and cemetery or the Francia estate area.

"Is there a problem, Justice?"

"In Buenos Aires men meet their *amantes* at hotels at noon."

"The theater is in the dining room."

He was out of the car and on the walk before I could get the keys from the ignition.

"Mary Ann and I did all the work. You and Justice had a study leave!"

Wilbur ducks the rubber band I flip. "Go heal the sick!" Pitching the book onto a shelf, I lean back into my reverie.

The War of the Triple Alliance, when Paraguay faced Brazil, Argentina, and Uruguay as joined adversaries, was fought 1865-1870. The participation of Argentina and Uruguay waned before the end, but Brazil continued the fighting, primarily because Lopez would not quit. Brazil repeatedly defeated Paraguayan troops and overran Paraguayan defenses and declared themselves victors. Lopez escaped with a few soldiers and rallied another offensive. At last the Brazilians caught him and Eliza Lynch with their sons as they fled north. They killed Lopez and his eldest son on the banks of the Aquidaban. Eliza dug shallow graves for them with her hands before she was returned to Asuncion and exiled, first to Buenos Aires and then to Paris where she died.

Paraguay survived as a country because of the jealousy Brazil and Argentina had for each other. But it lay devastated, stripped, and bleeding, reduced in size to national boundaries around an area the size of California. Reconstruction years were harsh. After the Brazilians left in 1876, Paraguayans resumed the self-government they had started in 1811. A succession of strong men, *juntas,* and governmental experiments marked 1876 to 1930. Another major war was fought in the 1930s between Paraguay and Bolivia over the Chaco, a vast wasteland between them marking the advance to the Andes, to settle a boundary feud going back to colonial days.

With the Spartan nature of the Paraguayans, the politically ambitious are always at odds with each other. Historically, whoever is in power exiles his opponents. A paradox is the welcome offered refugees from other countries. In the 1920s and 1930s the Mennonites, persecuted for their pacifism in Europe, were admitted by the thousands and given tracts of land in the Chaco to farm. From 1870 to 1920, thirty-two colonies were begun by foreign immigrants: Germans, Russians, Australians, British, and Italians. After World War II other foreigners have been the Japanese, as well as more Italians, Germans, and Spanish. A small Hutterite colony even flourished for awhile in the 1960s.

Shifting and changing governments have contributed to erratic development of the country. The last major revolution in 1948 brought to power the present administration which has attained a stability to allow the present progress.

A wall thermometer signals the cooler temperature of late afternoon. I move to the desk and begin to arrange the correspondence that must be answered. My eye strays back to the wood carving. I pick it up and rub the fine lines of the Indian's polished hair.

"Your children are many, *mi Cacique* ('my chief'). It helps to know about those of the past to understand those of the present. In two weeks I will visit one of your adopted sons and watch him create an image of a daughter of your blood. One day I shall take you both to my people for them to glimpse why I number myself with them and you as a citizen of two worlds."

2
In Social Customs

"Why do people stand at the gate and clap their hands?" I ask my hostess.

Mariana sits across the tea table from me in her sun-room. She shrugs her shoulders. "It is a custom. *Es costumbre!*"

I shake my head. "You sound like everybody else."

"So I'll invent you a story? We clap our hands at people's gates in winter to keep them warm and in summer to keep them cool. While we clap, we hope someone will come to the door and invite us in!"

"I thought you of all people would help me understand social customs." A dark beauty, she sits with the arched back rigidity of advanced pregnancy. Mariana Martinez, my friend, the wife of a general, who spent four years with him in Washington, D.C., while he was assigned to the Paraguayan Embassy, returns the gaze. With a fading laugh she sighs.

"I remember the confusion. Wanting to be accepted. Hoping to learn graces. Desiring the proper behavior." She counts the listing on her fingers.

"We can be insensitive in my country to those unlike us," I remark.

She is quick. "I loved living in the States! It hardly seems possible we have been back here a year. This is my first baby in Paraguay. The other children can claim American citizenship if they wish. This little one will have to settle for a *gringo* doctor."

My mind returns to the day we met when I was looking for a house to rent.

We had lived in the home of fellow missionaries, Bill and Fran Skinner, while they were on furlough. But they were returning, and the house next door to them destined for us was undergoing repairs. I met Mariana when she showed me a house for rent belonging to her and her husband. Though I didn't rent her house, we became good friends.

She moves in the chair and smoothes her dress. "You will have more babies? Your two still leave the house empty!"

"Someday."

"Someday!" She chortles. "I said to my husband he should be General Motors instead of General Martinez because he comes out with a new model each year!"

"Most Paraguayans do seem to have large families," I respond.

"It's . . . ," she pauses.

"*Costumbre!*" I add. We laugh.

"Lots of children are our way. That comes from the Church, from the way it has always been. The poor people look to their children to take care of them when they cannot care for themselves. In America, you have Social Security. Here, we have children!" Mariana explains.

"And old and young are together under one roof," I add.

"Sometimes it's only half a roof. No matter how poor we are, we do not turn out our old," she says proudly.

"What about privacy?" I ask.

"That is for poets and priests! Privacy is loneliness. We don't want it," she states emphatically.

I look past her shoulder through the open window to see the gardener bending over her flower beds. His movements take on the look of genuflection to an earth god.

"Would you be having your baby at the Baptist Hospital if you hadn't been to the States? Hadn't met me?" I ask.

"I like the new, the different. I would have gotten there eventually. But people do look at you with some suspicion," she answers.

"I know. That's why I need to understand the social customs,"
I continued.

"Like?"

"*Maté* gives me trouble."

"You don't like *maté*?"

"I love *maté*—in my own cup."

"In the old days, *maté* was the only beverage. It was our tea,
coffee, hot chocolate. But the time it was drunk was a close time, an
intimate time, almost a ritual. It is still a very common practice,"
Mariana explains. "We have *maté* like you have coffee breaks.
When people visit, the *maté* and *bombilla* are passed. It is a warm
time, a compliment to the guest.

"The *bombilla* is my problem. It bothers me to drink from the
same straw used by everyone else."

"You are bothered by the germ theory!" We laugh. "Many
people today do not offer the same straw and one cup."

"But many do."

"It is all right to refuse. People understand that foreigners do
not love *maté* the way we do."

"But to drink it as my hosts do would give me esteem and
respect."

"*Cierto* ('certainly'). You would immediately be *muy guapa* ('a
neat chick') the way we would say it. But maybe that which you
have gained as *la aficionada de los abrazos* will offset the *maté*."

My face colors. "You heard about that?"

"My gardener's brother works at the hospital. He told me."

"Was I scandalous?" I ask as my thoughts turn to the welcome
party when Wilbur and I first arrived.

With all the flourish and fanfare attendant on a Latin event, the
emcee for the party and all the men had eulogized and made
speeches with the great hugs, or *abrazos,* that is a custom for Latin
men. The hugging is accompanied by affectionate pats.

Feeling abandoned a bit and ignored a lot, at length I asked at a significant pause, *"No hay abrazos para mi*? ('Are there no hugs for me?')."

The emcee, a man of grace and charm, quickly corrected what I thought was an oversight, and I was hugged for the next hour.

"It would have been scandalous for me to have done it," Mariana says, interrupting my thoughts. "They loved it from you, talked about it for weeks. But I doubt you could get away with it again."

"Men hug men, women kiss women, and men and women shake hands," I state.

"Every time they meet."

"But men don't hug women."

"Only with their eyes."

Pabla, Mariana's maid, appearing with fresh tea, smothers a giggle behind my hostess. Mariana and I watch her set it on the table and retreat to the kitchen.

"My husband did something worse than I did with *abrazos*," I inform Mariana.

"That's possible?" she asks in mock disbelief.

"It happened when we went to the wedding of one of the nurses. Afterward, when all the people hugged the bride, a young man who works in the hospital office told Wilbur to hug, give an *abrazo,* to her. He was going to take a picture. Just as they hugged, someone walked between them and the camera."

Mariana bites a cookie and takes a drink of tea.

"The photographer told him to hug her again," I continue. "With great enthusiasm, Wilbur embraced her and said, *'Otro embarazo!'*"

Mariana spews her tea and catches it with a napkin. She holds her sides, laughing. "He didn't know *embarazo* was another word for pregnancy?"

"He does now," I laugh. "All through the wedding supper people explained to him the difference between *abrazo* and *embarazo.*"

"You think our weddings are different?" Mariana asks.

"Having two, the civil wedding and the one at church, was strange at first," I answer. "In my part of the States, we have receptions more than wedding suppers. We have rehearsal dinners for the people in the wedding the night before the ceremony."

"You rehearse a wedding?"

"Almost always."

"You North Americans and your organization!"

"I love the custom of *padrinos,* the couple that stands with the bride and groom. We have honor attendants, usually the best friends of the bride and groom."

"The *padrino* custom comes from our European influence. We are little mirrors of Spain, sometimes."

"Another custom I love is *siesta!*"

"For us, it is very practical. We get up early, before dawn, to start our work before the heat is severe. Winter is very short, but even then it is warm in the middle of the day. We sleep at the hottest time and work into the night when it is cool again."

"Aren't some people changing their attitudes about *siesta?*"

She nods. "A few keep working. But it used to be only new *gringos* who went out during *siesta.*"

"When we first came, I was downtown one day at noon and decided I would eat lunch and finish shopping when stores were open after *siesta*. But the lunchroom was closed for lunch and *siesta!* At least that place is open now at noon."

"*Siesta* affects work hours and meal schedules."

"I'd never make it up at three in the morning to drink *maté* the way the farmers do."

"You'd be ready if you went to bed at sundown."

I add, "I could eat the roll with them at mid-morning."

"Twelve thirty lunch is my first meal. I became decadent while we were in D.C."

We laugh. I look at my watch. "Tea at five in the afternoon is great for me, but it makes me worthless to prepare my family's evening meal," I comment.

Mariana offers a solution to that problem, "Have supper at ten at night like the rest of us."

"We have had to make some changes in the way we think of mealtime. I tried for a long time to get the women in my church to meet some time other than four to five in the afternoon," I explain. "They won't attend in the morning because they are doing their work. Early afternoon is siesta. They like the four to five hour because they can leave a snack and return to make supper."

"What did you do?"

"Sat by myself at my meetings until I decided to schedule the meetings when the women could and would come," I admit.

"Sounds like my husband having a Monday-night planning meeting for his staff in D.C. before he knew about football."

"Our *costumbre,* US style!"

Mariana asks, "Have you been to a *quince* yet?"

"We are invited to the one for Dr. Mendoza's daughter next month."

"They are such fun and celebration for a girl and her family."

"I was confused by the first explanation I had. I thought fifteen was too young to be engaged."

"In colonial days girls were married at fifteen, *quince,* or could be," she explains. "For her fifteenth birthday party, her chaperone, called a *duenna,* usually an older woman who was always with her, and her family celebrated the fact that she was old enough to have a fiancé. Now it is more like a debut, one of the passages of a girl to womanhood. She, officially, can date."

"The chaperone?"

"Those things are changing. But in some families a couple is accompanied by a third person, maybe a brother or a sister."

"I've been told that it is a practice to have a third person accompany a man and woman who are not married to each other. If I take a man somewhere in my car, for example, I should take one of my children or a friend with us," I state somewhat questioningly.

"People wouldn't think so much about you if you do not have a third person because you are North American, and we all understand that you have a lot of freedom. You could be with a North American man without a thought from anyone. You could be seen with a Paraguayan man too. But your husband should have a third person if he is with a Paraguayan woman."

"We know about that *costumbre*!"

"Already?" an amazed Mariana asks.

"The Baptist convention met in Encarnacion in July," I explain. "Our pastor's parents live there and his eighteen-year-old sister was up here with him and his family."

"Is he the German pastor?"

"Right. Elias Franz."

"Encarnacion is a long distance from Asuncion."

"Wilbur was planning to take some people from our church to the meeting. Alicia, the sister, and three others were going. Our pastor's wife told Wilbur she was sending her six-year-old daughter along."

Mariana points her finger. "Dr. Lewis's chaperone!"

"He was upset with her for doing that because he had the Volkswagen full."

"But that's the way it works. The six-year-old was the *duenna* for the eighteen-year-old," she nods knowingly.

"As we found out."

"Something happened?"

I continue my story, "The day they were to leave, for different reasons, the other three were unable to go. When Wilbur left with Alicia, he was glad the little girl had come. They rode in the backseat to be proper."

"That's it!"

"For two and a half hours they drove. Near sundown, just outside Quiindy, the Volkswagen threw a rod. They limped into town by struggling up hills and coasting down. A mechanic told them they'd either have to wait for parts from Asuncion or tow the car back."

"Did they stay there?"

"The mechanic told them a bus to Asuncion from Encarnacion

would be passing through anytime. Wilbur wanted to put the girls on it and send them back to Asuncion."

"Good plan."

"But the bus didn't show. You know how dark it gets in the country without electricity. The evening got colder and he decided he had to get them a place to stay. He found out later the bus never left Encarnacion. Another thing he learned later was that it was a record cold night for July. Encarnacion had frost."

"I remember that night!" sympathized Mariana. "Poor Dr. Lewis, stranded in Quiindy!"

"Getting a room in the rooming house was delicate. The host thought Alicia was Wilbur's wife and Esther his little girl and couldn't understand why he rented the room and went back to sleep in the VW."

"He didn't explain?"

"What could he say?" I ask. "Better the man thought they were married!"

"I'm sure the girls were frightened in a strange town, alone in a rooming house."

"Wilbur checked its safety and pushed a bed in front of the door. I had packed him a supper so they had some food. A blanket was in the car. He wrapped himself in it, pushed the front seat down, arranged himself in a Z, and tried to keep warm on the coldest night in Paraguay."

"How did they get out?" Mariana wants to know.

"Around eleven he suddenly remembered that Bill Skinner was leaving Asuncion at midnight with a carload of people planning to drive all night and arrive in time for the convention's opening the next morning. He calculated that Bill would be passing through Quiindy around two thirty in the morning."

"Nobody else would be traveling out there during those hours!"

"Near the time, Wilbur, looking like an American Indian in his blanket, went out to stand on the road. He hoped to send the girls on to Encarnacion with Bill if there were room, then he'd get the car back to Asuncion the next day."

"Dr. Skinner came?"

I nod, "He had Wilbur's problem. All his passengers had backed out except one lady. And he didn't even have a six-year-old!"

"But he came?"

"At last, way in the distance, Wilbur saw lights coming. It was Bill with his one lady."

"In the backseat!"

"Exactly. Wilbur didn't want to stop the car if it happened not to be Bill, so he stood just close enough to the highway that the lights would shine on him sufficiently for Bill to recognize him."

"It worked?"

"Bill saw him far away, but said, 'I'm not stopping for anybody.' His passenger said, 'That looks like Dr. Lewis.' Bill yelled, 'That is Dr. Lewis!' and screeched to a stop."

"I wonder who was happiest to see the other," observed Mariana.

"The problem then was to get the girls without waking up the town. He climbed over a fence at the back to get to the door he had barricaded for them."

"Good he got the right room."

"It terrified the girls to have a man calling to them to open the door at two thirty in the morning."

"But everybody got to Encarnacion?"

"And we even got the car back."

Mariana exclaimed "You understand about chaperones!"

I look at my watch again and begin to gather my things.

"This was fun. My house next time?" I ask.

"Next Thursday. Will you make me something?"

"Anything."

"A hamburger?"

"I'll teach you how to make them," I offer.

"I can't make them! Anyway, I don't want to know how," she explains. "They are no good unless a North American makes them."

"Tea and two hamburgers two weeks from today! Shall I come for you?"

"My husband will send a car."

"You are not driving now?"

"He'll send a driver."

We saunter and chat to the front gate. "You never did tell me why people clap at the front gate."

"It's a way to get attention. The gates don't have bells. The yards do have dogs! More than that, it's respectful. People won't enter your property without your permission."

"Even with the 'my house is your house' hospitality of people."

"'*Mi casa es su casa*' is the attitude in the response to the request for entry."

"Your *casa* has been a good place today."

We embrace. I get into my Volkswagen and turn it toward home. My home is their home too. Or maybe my home is a part of their house, their nation, that they have lent me for as long as I need it. Certainly, this rich culture is becoming my own.

Accelerating, I hurry—home.

3

In Missionary Medicine

She pushes a strand of hair inside her scarf and watches the people on the screen with unbelief etched in the lines that map her face. Light from the projector's beam spills over her features. Like tennis watchers, her eyes jump from the sight on the white square, to the projector, to Wilbur checking the inner parts of the machine, to the pastor standing beside him. I wonder if this is her first movie. That afternoon she had come to my station with the clinic.

On the pharmacy side of the truck, she took her place in line, holding the prescriptions in work-wrinkled hands as though they were documents of passage. She laid them on the counter with authority and said in mixed Spanish and *Guarani,* "First time in my life I see a *medico, un* doctor."

I looked at her card and read that she was thirty-six and had undergone a pregnancy each year for many of her childbearing years. Even I would have guessed her to be fifty. The fertility did not surprise me, nor did the fact that she had only seven living children from twelve pregnancies. Two babies had died as infants. She had miscarried three times. Turning, I began to prepare her medicines— a series of vitamins, iron, and something to kill her intestinal parasites. Her card noted that she needed three different surgical procedures to alleviate the problems caused by twelve pregnancies in twelve years. I knew she would never receive the total care she needed, and between the stark lines of the diagnosis I could read the frustration of my surgeon husband.

I chatted with her over my shoulder. "Do you live near here?"

"Two kilometers east."

"How did you know to come today?"

"My husband works far away in the town. A companion at his job is Baptist. He said his church asked the *gringo* doctor to come. My husband told me to come to see the North American doctor for my troubles. He sent me with our neighbor."

I handed her the medicines and explained how to take them. I added, "You did understand from the doctor that you need surgery?"

"I understand."

Her dress was clean cotton, colorless and frayed from its many washings. A slight stoop was scarcely discernible because of the erect tilt of her head. Graying black hair was smoothed back from her face and held by a scarf the blue shade of the national dyes, a cross between royal and navy. She wore it the way I have seen models wear scarves, with the three points to the back of the head and the two ends twisted and tied on top. But hers looked like the uniform headdress of the market women in Asuncion. The scarf and her brown-black eyes were the only color about her. She gazed back at me with only a nervous twisting of her hands on a fabric scrap handkerchief to betray any chink in her self-confidence.

I watch her animated face in the projector light. *Sure, you understand, I think. But you'll never get the surgery for the same reason that today is the first time you've ever seen an M.D. There is no care near enough to where you live and you can't go where it is available. For a while you will feel better with the vitamins and iron and worm killer, and you will believe in a miracle. You will say the pills of the* gringo *doctor cured you. When you have taken all the pills, you will know they didn't cure you. Then you will talk about the time when the kind North American asked you questions that surprised you and probed your body with gentle hands that had clean fingernails and went exactly where the pain was. His words about surgery will fade from your memory to be replaced by the miracle of temporary relief and the sight of movies. When the old pain and ailments return, strong as ever, you will think often of the brief encounter and it will be enough, for physical pain is life, and you really never expect to be free of it.*

In the afternoon I talked with her about her family. "Are your children healthy?"

"Yes!" Pride.

"Have they had their vaccinations?"

"Two have!" Smiles. Hope. Maybe the shots for two count something for the five who have not received anything.

I explained the urgency of their receiving inoculations. "Tell your husband there is a public health nurse who goes to the town where he works. She comes from the Ministry of Health in Asuncion. He can get information there and take the children to be inoculated."

"I bring them to you?"

"We will be in the village tomorrow at the Baptist church. If you can get them there, I will vaccinate them."

The excitement on her face is hypnotic. She is intent on the pastor's explanation of the movie, and the intensity of the expression never varies. *I must remember everything about you, Blue Scarf. You are the spirit and embodiment of rural Paraguay, stalwart, stoic, and even regal in your poverty and the odds against your survival. You ask for nothing and receive more from what is given than is really there.* I break from my obsession with Blue Scarf and turn to routine assignments.

Crowd counting during the movies is one additional chore in the job description of the pharmacist-nurse on our clinic trips. Missionaries work with loose reins, but two absolutes are to keep the financial records straight and send statistics back home.

I've never understood the numbers fascination in stateside churches. My suspicion is that counting the audience for an event is the indicator to prove ministry occurred. I've fought it with rebellion and cynical acquiescence. Now I just do it and look on counting the mobile clinic crowds the way I do paying bus fare to town. It's something I have to do to go on the trip. A small price, really, once I got some peace about the philosophy back of it.

I estimate a group of twenty-five, then eye-size a comparable group until I've "counted" the people seated around in the clearing. Two hundred fifty, maybe two hundred seventy-five, I reckon.

Reaching into a cabinet in the truck, I find an old towel I carry, my "stadium cushion," and spread it by the back right wheel of the clinic. Sitting on it, I lean against the tire. The pastor is preaching in *Guarani*. My mind wanders. This would be the concept of medical missions many of our friends in the States have. Of all we do, I love the mobile clinic trips most. I recall my favorite mobile clinic trip.

One Easter week we went to Pedro Juan Caballero, farthest town northeast on the border between Paraguay and Brazil, some two hundred and fifty miles off the paved highway. The Paraguayan Home Mission Board had requested we visit the towns and communities en route where there were either believers or people who were correspondents from the convention's radio Bible courses. We were also to initiate conversations with public officials, survey prospects for new churches, and offer free medical clinics as evidence of friendship and service. Our pastor, Elias Franz, also president of the Home Mission Board, went with us.

The second day out, Elias said to us, "I discovered last night that I didn't put my Bible in my bag. I will need to borrow one from you."

Wilbur sucked in his breath. "I didn't put mine in, either! I was so preoccupied with loading the truck!"

They stared at me. "I'm the nurse."

We named ourselves *los mensajeros de Samuel* for the rest of the trip in honor of the messenger in 2 Samuel 18 who ran to King David without a message. On the trip Elias developed a sty and eye infection. Arriving in Pedro Juan Caballero, he took the young pastor aside.

"Brother, do you have a Bible with large print that I may borrow?"

The trip was marked by scenery patterned after paradise. The green earth against blue sky was broken by sporadic color bursts from butterflies and birds that lined the sides of the road. We met and ferried across three placid rivers, the Piribebuy, Jejui, and Ipani, idyllic and unhurried, far to the east of the commercial Paraguay River, but feeding into it.

Near Pedro Juan, always alert to an opportunity to see some point of Paraguayan history, I talked my fellow messengers of Samuel into a detour to see *Cerro Cora* on the Aquidabán River, where Francisco Solano Lopez was killed as he and Madame Lynch and their children fled north by coach in the last hours of the War of the Triple Alliance. I knelt and touched the red clay of the river bank where Lopez and his oldest son, Pancho, were buried. A national hero, Lopez and his son are now interred in the National Pantheon, but *Cerro Cora* was his first shrine. It seemed to me the clay was darker red where I looked.

On the return trip, we took three side trips from the main road west to the Paraguay River and back to continue south. The first was to the towns Horqueta and Concepción, a principal river town in the north. The next was through the colony of New Germany to San Pedro, and the last was to Rosario.

Paraguay is divided into sixteen departments, and each is governed by a delegate appointed by the president of the republic. The departments are divided into municipalities and rural districts which are further divided into companies. Each district has a governing group of officials with the strongest being the *comisario* ("police chief") who is appointed by the central government in Asuncion. He and the locally elected *junta* carry out orders coming from Asuncion, as well as those arising locally. The *junta* elects a municipal president. The *comisario,* the *junta* president, and a judge appointed by the Department of Justice in Asuncion are the three most important people in town. Their offices are usually in the *comisaria,* almost always located on the plaza.

Our system was to roll into a town, call on the *comisario,* introduce ourselves, and tell our purpose for being there. We would get permission to announce and provide a free clinic on the town square in the afternoon and ask if we could show a religious film and preach a Bible message afterward. After announcing over the loudspeakers of the truck through the town that we were having the clinic and meeting, we located the people whose names had been given us by the Home Mission Board. With *siesta* past, we started the clinic and ran until dark, when we'd finish with films and preaching.

There was a sensitivity on the part of Paraguayan officials for the welfare of their people. We hadn't planned to hold a clinic in New Germany but did when the *comisario* came to the home of the believers where we were eating lunch and asked us to do so. There is a state prison at Concepcion. The governor of the department, or state, asked us to stay over a day and hold a clinic for the prisoners. Among others things, we diagnosed a case of leprosy!

Near the end of the trip, we began to get reports of bad weather. Roads are maintained by closing the unpaved ones when it rains. In spite of scurrying back to Coronel Oviedo, where paving began, we were rained in at a little town north of the barricade. Two Brazilian bankers traveling from Rio to Asuncion were also at our rooming house. They had managed to get a message to Asuncion for a plane to come for them the next morning. They suggested we go to the landing field with them and arrange with the pilot to return for us.

The landing field was a pasture. A four-passenger plane arrived as scheduled and landed after two low passes to clear the cows from the smoothest place. The pilot was amenable to returning for us, and an afternoon hour was agreed upon for us to meet at the pasture airport.

Dark, low-hanging clouds swallowed the tiny craft as we returned to our rooming house. Intermittent rain on the tin roof made rhythms according to the rate of the downpour. Sometimes it was a staccato beat that Gene Kelly or Fred Astaire could have entertained by and then it would switch to a lullaby or a hymn.

The hour arrived when we were to depart for the pasture. We

left our clinic truck safe but forlorn in the yard of our host, to be returned for when the roads were dry.

The rain let up, but on occasion brushed our faces like cat hair. We waited at our place with the ominous black clouds seemingly four feet above our heads.

And we waited.

Confident statements about getting back home and responsibilities turned to "What if?" and then, "Maybe he will come back tomorrow."

Before we gave way to despair, we heard a faint noise. The volume increased, and we finally recognized it as the motor of the little plane of our rescuer. After what seemed forever, a place in the clouds zipped open and out he popped. He taxied up to us and said we needed to hurry for he didn't want to take off in the rain. We were in the seats and braced for departure before he had finished his warning!

With bumps and rattles, we moved up and away through boiling clouds. Over air pockets and between lightning flashes we climbed. The feisty little engine groaned and, after several bouts of breath holding, we were above the clouds. A loud noise remained, but when I turned my attention to what it was, I found it to be the sound of my pounding heart in my ears.

The emergency of escape and takeoff faded. The next crisis was my fear of the escape vehicle. It did not seem as invincible in the air as it had on the ground. Windows rattled, knobs moved, seats wiggled. No flight attendant stood by to demonstrate or assure me of safety and emergency procedures. Through the intensity of my fright, I became aware of pain in my hands and looked down to see them, white-knuckled, locked unconsciously about the seat arms.

Gradually we moved out of the fiercest part of the storm. I looked furtively through cloud slits for smoke or other signs of civilization to head for *when* we crashed. Nothing on the control panel registered except a dial with a needle that moved steadily in reverse toward zero.

"What's that?" I whispered, nudging Wilbur and motioning toward the dial.

"That's the altimeter," he said, noting my wide eyes and dilated pupils. "When the needle reaches zero, a bell rings and the plane falls."

The needle reached zero. A bell didn't ring. The plane did not fall. Instead, it landed in sunshine in Asuncion, and we were soon back on familiar turf.

The night air cools. Standing, I feel in a drawer for my white cotton jacket and pull it about me. Arms folded, I sit and adjust to a comfortable position. Looking past the angle of the front wheel I see *Hospital Bautista* painted on the clinic truck's side and reflect on the work of the hospital.

Most of our medical work is carried on at the hospital. It is not a big institution by stateside standards, but we like to think of it as the "Mayo Clinic of Paraguay." With less than a hundred beds, it has the full services of medicine, surgery, obstetrics, pediatrics, emergency, and outpatient clinics. From admissions to wards, to surgery, to the patio gardeners, it is a community, a microcosm of people in league to do an immediate ministry to the body for a more lasting ministry to the soul and spirit.

The Paraguayan body suffers a variety of assaults on health. The most common problem is parasites. Some come through food but are controlled by thorough cooking. Our meat gets extra time on the fire to avoid problems with Trichinella in pork and basic bacterial impurities in beef.

Cats carry a variation of a Brazilian hookworm whose larvae cause problems for humans by infesting the skin. We are unable to let our children have cats for this reason.

A more exotic skin parasite is leishmaniasis. Wilbur had a patient from one of the tribes around Pedro Juan Caballero whose infection was so severe he nearly lost a leg from a bone-exposing ulcer.

The most common parasite is hookworm, which is transmitted from human to human. It is killed easily with medication, but it has not been controlled because people reinfect themselves by going barefoot in contaminated soil. The outstanding clinical problem with hookworm is anemia, as the parasite drains the hemoglobin from the blood.

Wilbur had a little boy with bleeding stomach ulcers, uncommon for a child and rare in Paraguay. He needed surgery but had only a four-gram hemoglobin count. Normal is twelve to fourteen. US medical texts indicate that people can't usually live with hemoglobin below five. With a combination of malnutrition, hookworm, and bleeding, the child was such a poor surgical risk that Wilbur could not operate. He talked to the father about giving blood. But Paraguayans are hesitant, even afraid to give blood.

He replied, "I cannot. I have to stay strong to work to feed the rest of my family. We are many."

There was no arguing that donating blood would not keep him from caring for his family. He believed he needed all of his blood to do that.

Wilbur told him, "Then we will give him blood from the blood bank, and I will donate my blood to replace the blood used."

The boy was transfused, given hookworm treatment, fed a high-protein diet, and given conservative, nonsurgical care for his ulcer. The bleeding stopped; he stabilized and responded to treatment. Surgery was eventually ruled out. The father was told all that had been done but believed that his son's cure was due to the blood of the strong North American, in spite of the explanation that it was not that precise blood his son received.

Transfusions are a problem here, not because of the receiving but because of the donating. The active surgical service and trauma care the hospital maintains necessitates a blood bank.

Stories, even legends, have arisen around the labors of Don McDowell, Wilbur's surgeon colleague, to procure and maintain blood for patient needs. One rather routine way of maintaining blood for the blood bank is having all the hospital employees typed and their information placed in a file. When a need arises, an employee with corresponding blood type is asked to give blood.

Once Don took blood from a husky, strong-looking patio worker. Upon standing, the man fainted, cutting a gash in his head when he fell. The first patient had to wait while the donor was carried around to have his head stitched.

Another time a man from one of the colonies came in and received extensive surgery with transfusions. Normal procedure when a patient needs a transfusion is for family and friends to donate the same amount of blood as the transfusion required. No family or friends had come to visit this patient. Don left word with the nurses that he should be notified at once if anyone came to visit the patient. At length, a visitor did appear, and Don scurried off to have the visitor donate blood. Afterward, in conversation, Don asked the man his relationship to the patient.

The visitor said, "I don't know him. He is from my colony. I came into Asuncion on business and met a friend downtown who told me he was out here. I just came by to see who he was."

With so many ethnic and foreign groups, we deal with dozens of languages. A characteristic of the work is the diversity of people. Usually there is some hospital employee who can translate whatever language a patient speaks. Once a man from one of the Mennonite colonies came to see Wilbur. It was late in the afternoon and the German-speaking employees had gone. The patient spoke no Spanish. Wilbur tried *Guarani,* Italian, and Russian to no avail. Finally, with lab tests, punch and jab, and good guesswork, he made a diagnosis. The next day in surgery, as he and the resident were scrubbing, he told the trouble he'd had making a diagnosis.

The resident said, "Dr. Lewis, I think he speaks English."

Wilbur marched from the scrub sink to the table where the patient was still awake. "Do you speak English?"

"Yes."

Another common medical problem is snakebite. Paraguay has many poisonous snakes. The venom of one of the worst works as an anticoagulant, or thinner in the blood.

A woman from south of Asuncion was brought in by her husband. He had found her by the woodpile where she had been chopping wood. She was in a coma. He thought she had had a stroke because she had a history of high blood pressure. She was being treated for stroke in emergency when one of the nurses noticed two little fang marks on top of her foot. She was given anti-sera, but then had a cerebral hemorrhage from the thin blood caused by the venom. Treatment was started for the stroke. Next day her leg swelled, turned black and blue, but she recovered eventually and was discharged.

I commented to Wilbur, "I'm sure her husband is delighted. No doubt the woodpile has gotten low with her being gone two weeks."

Missionary doctors practice medicine by shortwave radio with the New Tribes missionaries who are scattered all over the country in isolated areas. They are the only health care the Indians have. Their pilot flies emergency cases down to Asuncion. Wilbur once gave a two-day seminar during one of their mission meetings on recognition and treatment of more common conditions. Bill Skinner gets in on a lot of their radio calls because of things occurring with children. Two small tots took all their mother's thyroid tablets once. Bill kept in touch by radio until they were through the crisis.

The New Tribes missionaries started a work with the Maca tribe across the river from Asuncion, and Wilbur went to them every Thursday for a year. But the Indians would not come to the hospital. The missionary radioed Wilbur one afternoon to meet him at the river. A little girl in the tribe had a hematoma on her forehead that would not go away. Wilbur went, prepared to aspirate it, but found it had characteristics of a depressed skull fracture. He told them it was essential to bring her to the hospital for an X-ray. The next day, streaming into the hospital patio, came an entourage of the little girl, her parents, the tribal chief, and a dozen other people. Wilbur X-rayed, found a depressed skull fracture as he had suspected, and told them it would gradually heal in a couple of months without treatment, which is exactly what happened.

But the Indians believed the X-ray machine cured her. That

marked the end of their fears of coming to the hospital.

"*Sigan a Dios* ('follow God')!" The pastor makes an emphatic point and jolts me back into his sermon, past the fatigue and moonbeam chasing. I stretch and rearrange myself at my wheel post. I listen and follow until the *Guarani* goes past my understanding and covers me. I backpedal to Spanish, then English, and think of my attempts to follow God.

The hard part is not the following, but how to do it.

Deciding to be a medical missionary was easy. Deciding where to "med-mish" was the tricky part. We had to determine the continent, the country, and, in some instances, consider the different hospitals in a country.

There was the matter of compatible cultures. From my first contact with the Foreign Mission Board until I knew I'd be assigned to South America, I had intermittent qualms about being in an Oriental or Middle Eastern culture. I can barely survive the "submissive woman" emphasis in casual stateside contexts. I wondered how I could manage to be subdued and silent the rest of my life, which would be expected some places. The illogical reasoning of that was finally obvious. God would not give me the gifts I have then put me in a place to serve him where they could not be used. South America was no surprise. The expressive, emotional Latins suit me fine!

Baptist Hospital in Asuncion had a hospital base with active surgical service where Wilbur's training could be utilized. It had an integrated balance between social service institution and agent for church planting. The reputation of medical personnel was that of church planters, as well as medical missionaries.

" . . . *ensenandoles mientras se van,* ('teaching them as you go')" The pastor is preaching from the Great Commission. I stand and lean against the truck. The pressure lanterns around the

improvised pulpit cast stark light and deep shadow on the faces of
the people in front of the stand.
" . . . *ensenando, ensenando!* ('teaching, teaching')!"

We teach everywhere, especially in the hospital. The chaplain
conducts Bible studies in all the departments and has a full program
of ministry to the patients and their families. That's go-teaching,
done on the healing journey. The intern and residency programs
with scientific conferences have go-teaching to build up a national
profession. The medical staff Bible studies help those who are
believers and make friends for our work of those who are not. The
nursing school is go-teaching, and I'm a go-teacher in it.

"If you want to have Jesus, lift your hand. We will talk to you
some more, give you something to read, and leave you a New
Testament."
Blue Scarf, in a line between me and the projector, lifts her
hand. I blink tears and watch her with the pastor. She is the sum of
medical missions for me.

In the beginning I felt a defensiveness about being a medical
missionary because at times I sensed a suspicion from some people
in US churches because I had a performing skill. It was almost as if I
were not credentialed for the task because I did something other than
preach, and I went to the mission field almost apologetic for being
part of institutional missions. From there, for a time I viewed
medicine as a come-on, a bait to hook them into the kingdom!
But those who view service apart from evangelism miss the
heart of missions. And those who see evangelism as sufficient apart
from service miss the soul of the gospel. Opposing philosophies
melt out here in the front line of the battle.
Besides, the fish recognize the worms. In my days as a VA
nurse I worked on a medical ward where the patient census rose
dramatically with the first norther of the season when the winos and

street people hunted shelter. A man said to me as I did his admission interview one cold November day, "My buddy went down to that rescue mission, but I like it here better. You don't make me sing hymns."

I am at peace now with not expecting a payoff from people for what I give them. The physical and spiritual effects of pain can't be separated. I can preach to Blue Scarf about her need for Jesus. But she may be in so much pain from varicose veins and a prolapsed pelvis, so worried about food and education for her children, so preoccupied with her throbbing teeth, that she can't hear what I say or doesn't care about what I say.

Salvation is crucial, but alleviation of pain is more immediate. If I involve myself in her pain, she hears. For while pain is preeminent, belief is more powerful. Medicine gives me a shortcut between the two.

Missions is incarnation. God did it first in Jesus. I do it now in the body God gives me to stand with these people in their country, culture, and langauge, living God as best I can in front of them. My incarnation promises nothing, guarantees nothing, except that obedient belief in God stands incarnate in the midst of a people. I stand and wait to serve and be.

The three of us jolt over the rough road to the place where we will eat and sleep. We agree on having a good day and clinic.

"I have a confession," I say. "When I put away our gospel tracts, I couldn't find our record book."

The pastor is consoling. "It will appear."

Wilbur adds, "Just keep a rough idea to enter in the log book. How many were there? *Muchos!*"

"One," I correct him.

"One?"

"She wore a blue scarf."

4
In National Churches

With the last chord and a lingering amen intended to induce reverence, I stand from the pump organ and take my seat on the front pew to listen to the sermon. Before Wilbur can get to the pulpit, Don Basilio asks if he may have *la palabra* ("the word").

"Of course," Wilbur answers. Our brother, whose forebears held Russian citizenship, launches into his weekly diatribe.

I settle back and search for a place to put my eyes. I learned long ago that, if I look at him, he is encouraged by what he considers to be my interest. I gaze at the baseboard below the window, see a colony of tiny black ants, and fix on them with a consuming interest.

When Wilbur and I returned from furlough and started the church in Sajonia as a mission of our home church in Fernando de la Mora, our fellowship met in Don Basilio's home for a few weeks until he made it clear he preferred that we move on. I think I precipitated that by not listening to his preconversion stories of personal sin. I had heard them so many times I could have repeated them antiphonally with him. At first I thought I was serving as some sort of confessor in his efforts to purge himself but soon realized he was just reliving vicariously the last excitement his life had held. He got more points for disavowal because he was renouncing his sins to a missionary. A few times were acceptable; but after three months I realized we were dealing with joys remembered instead of sins forgotten.

The ants are busy carrying burdens from an origin I can't see to

a destination I am unable to detect. The puzzlement I feel in
watching them matches that which I have felt at times in the past in
trying to decipher church life here.

Our family joined the church in Fernando de la Mora our first
term on the field. Located in the first town east of Asuncion, it was a
stable, growing congregation with a Paraguayan German pastor and
a warm fellowship. With a full church program and national
leadership, we felt we would be better equipped to spend our first
years in such a church, learning, before we struck out on our own.

We learned! I learned how to be a children's worker (I'd never
worked with children in my life); how to be a Vacation Bible School
director and how to have VBS at Christmas (December is vacation
time and people love Bible schools and revivals at Christmas). We
learned how to get to Sunday School at 8 AM (We came early
because of the heat in the hot weather and to stay in the habit when it
was cold weather) and how to survive two-hour business sessions
(Everyone speaks on every issue since church is the one place where
members can say what they think and be heard.). We learned how
close to build the outhouse to the window where the pump organist
sits (In the heat the odor is distracting, in cooler weather, the view!);
how to have a workday at church (On holiday workdays, the men
repaired and built, the women cleaned and cooked, and I, with a car,
fetched and carried.); and how to love a group of people who
became the visible, tangible family of the Father, the body of Christ,
on that gravel street.

They covered and forgave my learning mistakes. They endured
my crusades. The Lord knows how much they covered, forgave, and
endured! I am not sure of all of it yet. They helped me birth a baby
and cried when I took her away on furlough because she was
Paraguayan, theirs.

Pastor Elias, one of the finest shepherds I have ever had, was
married to Dona Blasida, a warm and loving sister. A philosophy of
life that I still cling to came from her.

The women's meetings were often half used with "if onlys" and "what ifs." At a strategic point, she said once, *"Bueno, hermanas, tenemos que conformarnos a lo regular y seguir adelante."* ("Well, sisters, we have to conform ourselves to the average and forge ahead.")

I squint at the ants. They are carrying small particles of the wall on their minuscule backs. My church wall!

The Russian sounds as though he is winding down. I risk a look.

"And so, we must exhort each other to be pure and faithful and our pastor must give us the example." He throws Wilbur a defiant look and marches to his seat.

Wilbur thanks him for "the word." "Our brother is right that we should exhort each other, and I hope to give an example. However, exhortation should be done in the spirit and love of Christ, with the aim of building up each of us that we, his body, may stand."

I beam and give my attention to the pulpit and its occupant, ignoring the ants, as I remember our beginnings in this church.

When we returned from furlough, we talked to the church in Fernando about beginning a work in Sajonia, the oldest part of Asuncion. With Fernando as the mother church, the Russian's family, another family of believers, and four students from the theological institute, the work was officially opened with a Vacation Bible School which I directed. One hundred and seven children, one hundred and one of whom had never been to church before, met for Vacation Bible School in the modest home of Lili, the wife and mother in the other believer family. For numbers lovers, it was an astounding success. I thought it was a mess, except for the fact that it got the attention of the neighborhood, and Irma was saved.

Irma was sixteen when her aunt, a friend in another church, brought her to my house.

"She is very intelligent. She comes from the country to go to

school. I want to put her with a family so she can have a job and a
place to live. I knew you were returning with a baby, so I saved her
for you."

She was wonderful. It was love at first laundry.

When I prepare VBS, I create it all over the house. Some
families have to care for mothers who suffer from migraine. Mine
deals with a VBS director. They step softly, watch what they move,
and never ask anything that requires any concentration to answer.

One day the week before my grand opening VBS of the Lord's
work in Sajonia, Irma came into the kitchen and stood watching me,
neck deep in activity materials.

"*Senora.*" Softly.

"Yes?" Distractedly.

"How do you do what your book says? How do you be a
Christian?"

She had my instant attention. I gave her the full plan and then
some.

"I have already done all of that."

"How? When?"

"I read your books after I did my work."

"You know you need Jesus to be right with God?"

"Yes."

"You have confessed your need and desire to be reconciled
with God? You have asked him to come into your life?"

"Yes."

"You have prayed to God about this?"

"Yes."

"Do you have a Bible?"

"No."

"I will give you one. I will show you a book in it called the
Gospel of John. Begin reading it. Go to the church across the road
on Sunday and tell the people that you have personal faith in God
through Jesus. They will send you to the new believers' class. When
they consider you ready, they will baptize you and you will be a

member of the church. But you are a Christian now because of your belief and trust."

Three months later she was baptized and became a member of the church.

I look across the aisle at Lili and the Lomaquis family. Mr. Lomaquis is a giant among Paraguayans. He is Wilbur's height, six feet, and at least fifty pounds heavier. I remember the first time I saw him. Lili and I walked into a neighborhood store one Saturday during our visitation time to invite the family to church. The business belonged to Mr. Lomaquis. He reached under the counter, pulled out a Bible, and held it before us.

"I have one of your books. It fell into my hands from the sky."

The Lomaquis family had lived in the Chaco. On a Sunday morning thirteen years before moving to Asuncion, Mr. Lomaquis heard an airplane with engine trouble circling overhead. He put out a bed sheet to show the pilot where to land. When the plane was safely on the ground, three grateful Anglican missionaries climbed out. First came a man and his wife who was about to have a baby. The third person was a single woman. They were headed to Asuncion where the couple's baby was to be born. Only the single woman spoke Spanish, as the language in the area of their mission was an Indian dialect. They desperately needed to radio to their people for extra engine parts. Mr. Lomaquis knew of a radio about five hours away by horseback. He also knew within that approximate period of time the radio would be sending and receiving messages for the week.

There were no roads. Of the three, only the single woman had ever ridden horseback. Mr. Lomaquis saddled two horses and away they raced against time. After four hours, he realized they would not make the call schedule unless he went on alone. The woman agreed to stay at a ranch. Hurrying ahead, he reached the radio in time to send word to the fellow missionaries of the stranded three. He went back to get the young woman, and together they returned to his home. By the following morning, help had come and the three were on their way to Asuncion where the baby was born. As the three were going back to their station, they stopped at the Lomaquis house and gave them the Bible.

In his testimony before the church prior to his baptism, Mr. Lomaquis said, "That is how the Bible fell into my hands from the sky. But it didn't really mean anything to me except as a nice remembrance from some people for whom I had immediately developed a liking. As time went by, my family and I moved to Asuncion. I gave the Bible to my mother-in-law.

"I have always been interested in the religious beliefs of people and freely talk with anyone. One day while I was at my mother-in-law's house, I saw the Bible, dust-covered, in a corner. It made me remember the lovely experience of my friends from the sky, so I took it home and began reading it at the beginning. I was shocked and appalled at the cruelty and barbarity and wondered why people thought it was such a great book. So I left it for awhile and have recently begun to read it with more interest and understanding."

He went on to tell about our visit and how he began attending the church.

"I have trusted Christ and studied the doctrines of my church during my indoctrination classes. To fulfill the commandments of Christ, I want to be baptized."

"The commands for love and faithfulness are twin mandates." Wilbur is illustrating the first part of the sermon. I follow his line of development. Our people love to hear Wilbur preach, not because of his sermons but in anticipation of what he might say. I glance about the worship group and see faint smiles on faces. They are pleased by what they are hearing. Or maybe they are remembering the husband of the hen.

While we were still meeting in the rented house, Wilbur preached a series of sermons on the life of Christ. When referring to

Peter's denial, he could not think of the word for rooster, *gallo*, so he communicated by describing it. He called it *la gallina macho* ("the male hen") and, then, to avoid any possible misunderstanding, added *el esposo de la gallina*, ("the husband of the hen").

Another time he preached an entire sermon on the second coming of Christ as the second avenue of Christ.

My favorite was an episode that occurred during a series of messages on the miracles of Christ. Wilbur was trying to explain faith healers to people who have had little experience with that phenomenon. He first talked about radio preachers.

"In my country, there are preachers on the radio who say, 'Send me your diapers,'" and he used the word *panales*, instead of *panuelos* for handkerchiefs.

The front row of little kids who sat through each service swinging their legs, playing, and kicking each other, stopped stone still. The congregation stared ahead with mouths twitching.

Wilbur backed up, realizing he was not communicating his intention, and made his statement again saying "diapers."

The little ones giggled.

"Look," he said, picking up a handkerchief from the table pulpit, "Someone left his diaper here."

"Panuelo!" I whispered from my seat at the organ. We all took a couple of minutes from the worship for a hearty laugh.

I look toward Luis at the end of my pew. He is the oldest of eight children and lives with his mother to the east of the church in the ghetto area on the riverbank. The Sosa family lives near him, and they brought him first to our fellowship. He is president of our youth group. I was skeptical of him at first because of my experience with Serafina.

Closing my eyes, I see that lovely, innocent face.

Serafina attended services a couple of weeks, then waited for me one Sunday night.

"*Senora,* I would like to talk to you. I am embarrassed to talk to the pastor."

"Certainly."

"I have lived where I can because I have no parents. My father's brother let me live with him and his family in the country, but a month ago he said I must find another place. A relative of my mother let me come to their house here. I heard about the church and decided to find out for myself. *Senora,* I have looked all my life for what is here."

"That's wonderful, Serafina. Is there any way I can help you?"

"No, no. I just want to say to you how happy I am that you are here."

She was back on Wednesday night. I drove her home. We sat in front of her house, and she told me a lovely story of longing after righteousness and searching for God. I could hardly wait for furlough to repeat it!

On Saturday Lili went with me to visit her. We left misty-eyed and rejoicing over such a beautiful, sweet girl whom God had sent to us to nurture and guide in the faith.

The following Saturday, we took Justino, our associate pastor and theological institute student, with us to call on her. Lili and I were exuberant afterward. Justino was subdued.

The next day Serafina was not at church. I mentioned it to Justino.

"I told her I was speaking to the young people in Mario's church last night."

"Your classmate?"

"Yes. She was there. I introduced her to him. I think she went to hear him preach today."

Two weeks passed, and I went to her house. No one was at home. The fourth week, the lady of the house greeted me.

"She moved away. I do not know where." Her answers were curt.

Another week passed. On Wednesday night, Justino said to me,

"My classmate, Mario, has left the institute."

"Why?"

"He and Serafina have moved in together."

Aghast, my mouth dropped. Later, with the surprise lessened, I asked Mariana, "Why did she behave as she did with me?"

"She wanted something from you."

"But I offered to help her get a job and help her enter the nursing school."

"She wanted a man."

"I have no man to give her!"

"But you know important men. She thought she could meet one through you."

The next week Luis appeared with the Sosa family. He was sweet and enthusiastic! I watched him guardedly, wondering what he wanted from us. But he has progressed well through the early steps of faith.

The service is coming to a close. I feel the sermon winding down and look again at the ants. They have made a hole all the way through the plaster during the worship hour. I must put something on them when I come back to clean the church tomorrow.

"If you want to take the step of faith, come as we sing our closing hymn."

I go to the organ and accompany a hearty rendition of "Just As I Am."

"Pastor Justino will lead us in a prayer of worship before the offering."

While Justino prays, I squint and open the Thompson Third Grade music book.

I am not a musician, but I am all that we have. I cannot play all hymns. I don't like to play a hymn we can sing for an offertory, processional, or recessional. With some meditative consideration of the kids' piano books, a chord here and there, and a proper amen, we had some fine fill-in music.

The service is over. Nonmembers leave, the children get situated outside with a tree to climb, and the members reconvene for business meeting.

Wilbur convenes the group. "Pastor Justino will give the organizational reports."

I shuffle papers, knowing I will be next with the treasurer's report. All Sunday afternoon I record and balance my book. On Monday afternoon I go downtown and stand in lines to pay bills.

Our record system is a yard square fabric with pockets the size of offering envelopes. I assign a number, one through fifty, to each member and have each envelope marked and in its pocket on Sunday morning. A person gets his envelope, puts in his tithe, and I record the tither and return the envelope to its pocket. One box of envelopes lasts us a year, unless we have a spurt in church growth. The idea is from Fernando. Its refinement is mine.

Although I have more paper than money, I work hard at the assignment. Once while on furlough, Leanne looked at the extensive pages of the church financial report, was surprised, and said, "When did you do this?"

"That is all of our business. I would like to ask Brother Lomaquis to give a report on plans for the inauguration." Inauguration services are held when a new church is founded or when a church moves into its own building. Lottie Moon funds paid for the property and materials for our new church building.

"Pastor, the committee reports these plans for our inauguration. Dona Lili is in charge of invitations to all the sister churches. Pastor Justino is inviting the program personalities, and Don Basilio's family and mine will host the social time afterward. Pastor Justino will report on the program."

Justino details the welcomes, sermons, and music. The big event, a month from today, is a special event for me. There is no joy quite like helping birth a church. I plan to be in the middle of this occasion. At least twice before, I felt like I was on the sidelines.

The Billy Graham Crusade in Paraguay happened our first six months on the field. I was so new in the work that I felt I hardly counted. The team did come to my house for lunch, and I bragged about it until Mariana asked, "What's such a favor in that? You cooked them a meal. Why shouldn't they show up?"

I did sing in the choir. And one night, Billy, turning to look at us, winked at me. But the missionary next to me spoiled it.

"Did you see that?" She grabbed my arm. "He winked at me!"

At the time of Paraguay's phase of the Crusade of the Americas, I was in bed with hepatitis.

Wilbur came in one day and said, "The Crusade Committee is making a visit to the president of the country and will present him a gift. We wondered if you will wrap it."

I spent most of an afternoon carefully preparing a large plaque in shiny red paper and gorgeous bows, after scrubbing my hands so thoroughly I could see my blood through transparent skin. No gift was ever prepared with such a sense of divine calling. I was eager to have a report.

"How was the visit?" I asked Wilbur.

"Oh, fine. Why did you put so much tape on the gift? He could hardly open it."

"Is there any miscellaneous business?" Wilbur is bringing things to a close.

Strolling to the car, I talk with people and wait for the children. With a backward look I see Wilbur detained by Don Basilio.

I think of the ants. They will destroy our beautiful building by chipping and biting away at it. Don Basilio may do the same thing. It is a strong building. We can control the ants. Don Basilio is God's responsibility.

Wilbur gets in the car, and we head toward the avenue.

"What was Don Basilio's problem now?"

"He said I exhorted too much in the sermon about things I don't understand."

We bounce along on the cobblestone street.

"I have a sermon text for you next week."

"What?"

"Proverbs 6:6. 'Go to the ant, O sluggard; consider her ways and be wise.'"

"Good idea."

"My idea is not the approach you'd expect."

"I knew it wouldn't be."

5
With the Missionary Spouse

Siesta is not nap time for me. It is catch-up hour on my English magazines. The Oklahoma WMU sends us *Time* and *Ladies' Home Journal*. Sixty minutes inside their covers bring America in my house for a visit.

The current issue of the *Journal* lies open on my abdomen and I stare at the ceiling with my hands behind my head, stretched on the bed to get the benefit of the quiet hour. I contemplate the latest feminist article and count the ventilation holes in the ceiling squares.

Is there a conspiracy against women in the male workday world? More likely, it's an unconscious arrogance. It would rarely enter the mind of the average man that a woman could do his job as well as he, let alone improve on it.

The truth is, women do many things much better than men. Apart from the women who have stormed the bastions of traditionally masculine professions, there has always been a group who have consistently bested the men of any category—wives. Anybody knows who keeps the pastor going. In a nitty-gritty argument, what lawyer ever bested his wife? Who is the nurse for the sick doctor?

Women do seek careers. But the activists who insist that every woman should look outside herself for expression or consider herself a dolt simply call attention to their own inadequacies in spite of testimonies of self-fulfillment.

I'm caught in a dilemma on this. Few career women work harder than I do. At least a dozen jobs claim me. But many of those with whom I work closest consider me "just a housewife." That may be how I view myself.

The only part of the subject that might push me to wage a crusade is the terminology. I don't like the word *housewife*. I would prefer something more descriptive of the way I feel about my life's work—something exotic like artist in residence, or family architect, or creative arbitrator, at the very least *homemaker*. But men, the guardians of tradition, are not excited by such phrases.

Recent evidence is the series of courses on cooking, child care, and kindred subjects we offered at the church last month. We discussed a name for it.

"I think we should call it The Domestic Art and Science." Since I was teaching it, I felt my preferences should be heeded.

Wilbur, predictable husband, and Justino, unmarried, thought The Domestic Course would be better. We settled for lack of vision and called it The Course.

Sometimes the blahness of terminology permeates the lives of women and robs us of the glamour and excitement of what we really are.

Exhibit A is my own situation. I read the pamphlets on missionary job descriptions. The images they conjure up are so exciting! Then I read the one on the missionary homemaker. Yuk! I never can decide what person with which bias wrote it.

Missionary homemakers form the largest missionary category on the mission field. Surely the Foreign Mission Board is aware that the key to success or failure of the missionary enterprise lies in the hands of women.

I turn on my side and look out the window at my trees. Do I get any credit anywhere for being a tree planter? Maybe with God. Other than being saved, having a call of the Lord, a certain amount of study beyond high school, and being married to a prospective missionary, few prerequisites are written for the potential missionary wife. Why would there be extra credit for the gift of tree planting?

A wife can almost get to the mission field on her husband's coattails. But can she stay? She can if she is smart, studies a lot, catches on quickly, and has a tree to climb in once in a while!

I punch a pillow under my head and watch a fly crawling on the outside of the screen while I compile a list of the various fields of study to help the prospective missionary homemaker.

Theology. A missionary wife doesn't absolutely need a Master of Divinity degree, but she ought to be able to whip up an acceptable thought or two if her husband can't get to prayer meeting. She should be able to do simple things—like lead a women's study on the biblical basis for missions.

She will need some background for personal visitation to answer with tact, but authority, questions about the difference between what she believes and what Catholics, Jehovah's Witnesses, and Mormons believe, as well as Methodists, Presbyterians, and Disciples of Christ. She ought to be up on current ecumenical thought enough to know how to cooperate and with whom.

Naturally, she will need to be able to hold forth with furlough speaking in a way inspiring both to the sophisticated and the humble.

She must know how to be gracious in the face of deputation discrimination. If a male missionary talks in a church service, it is called "preaching." If a female missionary talks, it is called "speaking." After careful observance, I have discovered the difference. When a male missionary "preaches," he receives a love offering. When a female missionary "speaks," she receives a devotional book. As far as I am concerned, paying a missionary with a devotional book is like paying your doctor bill with Band Aids.

Some theological study will be essential for her own needs. Sooner or later she will abruptly ask herself one day, What am I doing here anyway?

Teacher Training. Some of us must teach our own children. After two attempts at the Calvert kindergarten course, I am convinced that generally, few mothers can teach their own children. There is a period for the child when the mother is the most effective teacher, but this usually ends with the preschool years. When our

youngest said, "I'm not going in that 'bigger garden,'" I accepted it
as a wise saying and let the matter drop. Perhaps there will be a
remedial kindergarten course offered at her college. However, many
mothers do teach their children and are even quite successful.

Calvert is wonderful. But some things are lacking. Example:
Mother-Teacher: "Today we are going to plot a train trip from
Providence to Buffalo."

Missionary Child Who Has Spent Two Furlough Years at Four-
Year Intervals in the Southwestern US: "Mommie, I mean, Teacher,
I know what a buffalo is, but what kind of an animal is providence?"

If a missionary couple is going to a field where the mother will
teach her own children, she should not economize on preparation in
the teaching field—even to graduate study, if she feels she should,
in order to have the confidence and security she needs to teach her
children. She might even be able to use her training to direct a
school for missionary children.

If a couple will be going to an area where the wife will not be
responsible for her children's schooling, the educational requirements suggested for her in the brochure are adequate. If she needs
extra training for ancillary teaching that any missionary wife does—
Sunday School, Church Training, Vacation Bible School, women's
groups—she can perhaps rely on correspondence courses.

Medical Skills. A number of missionary wives are nurses.
Those who aren't should not leave the continental United States
without a passing knowledge of how to differentiate symptoms of
the three most common medical problems.

(1) Classifying a fever: Is it bacterial or viral in origin? If it's
any comfort, most medical doctors have not mastered this puzzler.
After incisive, deliberate study, I have isolated the prevailing
philosophy: When in doubt, call it a virus. A virus can't be seen
under an ordinary microscope, so no one can prove it isn't a virus.

Is it more like flu or the beginnings of dengue fever? Flu is a
good guess unless one is living in a dengue fever area. Even so, it
still could be flu.

Should it be isolated or chalked up to too much birthday party? (The only truly isolated children are those who are restrained [tied] in beds on hospital wards.)

(2) Classifying vomiting: Is it the onset of appendicitis (serious) or the herald of pregnancy (more serious)? Is it the beginning of hepatitis or the result of a trip to the open market?

(3) Classifying diarrhea: Is it chronic (every day) or acute (every day and night)? Is it endamoeba histolytica (hard to treat) or emotional (impossible to treat)?

In the United States many act sick, but outside our native land the missionary wife will discover that almost everyone *is* sick. She will need to be able, in casual contacts, to instruct about hygiene, child care, and routine health precautions. The wife who wants to pursue this interest further can graduate to community and regional health teaching, well-baby clinics, and public health.

If for no other reason, the missionary wife should be well versed in basic medical knowledge because of her own needs. The world's worst patient is a husband. Next are children.

Home Economics: So obvious is this need that it might seem superfluous to mention. It is logical that a wife have the basic skills, but there are deeper needs.

(1) Cooking: A missionary wife must know how to cook from scratch. And if she wants to maintain her emotional health while on the field, she will scrupulously avoid magazines with pictures of luscious meals whose recipes read, "Take one can of . . . , one package of . . . , set automatic oven. . . . " On furlough, of course, she should cook no other way.

(2) Sewing and tailoring: The pattern instructions may be right and pure. But the missionary wife has to know how to redo the contents of the missionary barrel. The contents may not be clothes, but they are material. I have figured out how to use practically everything from our barrels except two left shoes.

In redoing the barrel, the missionary wife should, by all means, keep up with fashion. There is nothing more demoralizing to a missionary woman than to look like the stereotype. There's nothing wrong with feeling like one, if that's what leads to happiness. My own morale is better if I neither look nor feel like my own mental stereotype of a missionary.

(3) Interior decorating: A missionary couple can take a lot of things to the field but never all they will need. A wife must learn to work with what is available in order to get a result akin to a photo from *Better Homes and Gardens*. She must be careful not to be too successful, however, lest visiting dignitaries from the States think missionaries are overpaid.

Business Management: In her role as business manager, the wife will need to master many areas.

(1) Hotel service: The missionary home is a haven for the family and a hotel for everyone else. Strangely, most missionary wives actually enjoy this aspect—within reason. No one knows the joy of friendship and visiting, especially if the visitors speak English.

But when the baby has a cold, the sheets from last night's visitors are still on the bed, the ten-year-old needs a costume for a play, and a program must be prepared for the church meeting tomorrow, and her husband calls to say, "Honey, Dr. X is in town for two days. OK if I invite him to stay with us?" . . . Well, it's hard to remember 1 Peter 4:9.

(2) Catering service: In many mission areas, churches use holidays for workdays at church. This usually involves a meal at the church. While everyone else works on the church, the missionary wife works on preparing food for the workers.

(3) Parties and meetings: The missionary home sometimes resembles a community social center. It is the locale for meetings of every sort and parties of every size. My record sit-down dinner was served to fifty-seven people. Small, intimate functions of six to eight people don't seem challenging anymore.

(4) Paying bills: The physical side of business management usually becomes second nature to a missionary wife. The financial side is another matter. Even the national currency becomes fun. To

take a twelve-inch stack of paper money and divide it into little piles for specific bills is to pretend you are very rich.

Personal Interests: The successful (i.e., sane), missionary wife will discipline herself to leave a bit of time for her own interests. Painting, ceramics, writing, gardening, sports, whatever it is, she should pursue it. Even if it seems ridiculous, if it relaxes her, renews her perspective, she should do it.

Miscellaneous: (1) Musical ability: The missionary wife doesn't need a lot of musical training because in many areas little will be known about music. If she is too well prepared, she will only be frustrated. If she is planning to teach music, of course, that is another matter. But if she can just play hymns up to four sharps and four flats, she will be fine.

A bit of background in composition would be helpful to change the hymns to fit the occasion, such as weddings, funerals, and luncheons. Music theory would be valuable, too, so she can construct chords for all the choruses the people know.

If I am ever put in charge of everything, one thing I plan to demand is that stateside seminaries include a course on reducing all unknowns to the key of C.

(2) Secretarial ability: The skill is invaluable to all the correspondence, church, Convention, and Mission work the wife expects to do. It is also invaluable for all the correspondence, church, Convention, and Mission work she does not expect to do. A short legal course with any secretarial training would be a wonderful adjunct for understanding Mission documents and parliamentary procedure.

(3) Public relations: Any help along the line of personnel management, public speaking, and public relations would stand the wife in good stead with nationals, missionaries, and hired help. It is always great to know all one can about the government and history of the host country, as well.

(4) Psychology and counseling: Armed with a little psychology know-how, a wife can care for herself, her family, and others.

(5) Cosmetology: The smart wife won't set out to win the

world and lose her husband. Stringy hair and careless appearance can put a strain on the biblical mandate for a man to love his wife as his own body.

(6) Carpentry, electricity, and mechanics: A missionary wife can do what she wants with these skills. If a man wants to tend to these areas, don't deny him the privilege. But when he is not around, the sharp wife will manage to get the essentials done.

Above all, she should know how to change a flat tire without letting anyone know she can do it and learn how to say, "The gas tank is empty," in the language of her host country.

I sit up on the side of the bed and rub my shoulders. Looking in the mirror, I congratulate myself on a noteworthy job description.

It may sound like an impossible list for the missionary wife to master. But three-fourths of the fun is the trying.

6
In Missionary Home Life

Humming happily, I dab perfume behind my ear. I glance in the mirror and see Wilbur's approval reflected from his eyes.

"A birthday is such fun," I say.

"When it's mine and I take you out to dinner to celebrate?"

"How else?"

The phone rings. My joy falls into my shoes and anchors me. He crosses the room. *"Hola. Si."*

I quit listening to the words. The tone of his voice tells me the evening is canceled. He hangs up the phone and turns.

"Honey, I'm sorry. It's my night on. There's been a bad accident, and the resident needs help."

Managing a tight smile, I nod.

"I may not be long. Maybe we could go later."

"Sure, fine."

He throws off his suit coat, snatches a white jacket, and jabs his arms in its sleeves while going down the hall in his emergency half-run.

Staring in the mirror, I hear the slam of the front door and feel it like a slap. With eyes squinted tightly together, I will away disappointment's tears.

"He won't be back," I say to the mirror. "And I'm hungry." I head for the kitchen.

"Mother!"

"Karen?" I look in the front bedroom.

"I thought you and Daddy went out."

"He had to go to the hospital for a while."

"He won't be back," Karen states.

"Mommie?" A voice calls from the opposite bedroom.

"Leanne?" I tease, mimicking her tone.

"Will you lie down with me?"

"OK. Scoot." I always marvel at the power in the monosyllables. OK. Scoot. Hush. Hurry. Here. Yes. No. Shhh. Lying beside her on the ridge created by twin beds pushed together, I try to avoid wrinkling my dress, just in case. She snuggles close.

"Tickle me on my poopabutton."

"Oh, no! I couldn't do that!" And I reach for her middle and lightly jiggle my fingers on her navel.

Three-year-old arms and legs flail in the next bed. "Giggle me, too, Mommie!" Cristen's face hangs over mine.

"Why aren't you two asleep?"

"We're listening," says Leanne, the one in charge.

"To what?"

"The night, and for you and Daddy to leave."

"The night says you are keeping it awake! And Daddy and I aren't going after all."

"Giggle me, Mommie!"

"Where do you want to be giggled?"

"On my gully-gully!"

I tickle her throat under her chin to the music of her laugh.

"Let's tickle Mommie!" A chubby arm hits my hairdo from Pepe's and a bigger arm thrown around my neck smears my lipstick. After awhile I relax with them and the primitive heat of maternity eases my earlier tensions. Soon their regular breathing and soft kitten snores tell me they are asleep. I disentangle myself and cover them with a sheet.

With hunger more insistent, I resume the trip to the kitchen. David is peeking out the door of his room. He makes big eyes at what remains of my glamour. A second exposure to masculine admiration in one evening is too much to resist.

"Hey, old Dave, how about a date? We'll get Karen and have Daddy's birthday cake and tea by candlelight in the kitchen."

I put water on to heat and rummage in a drawer for candles. "David, you may light the candles. Karen, get some of our china from the dining room. We'll have a real party."

With faces softened by mellow candlelight, we sit, sip, and eat chocolate cake. Karen looks at the results of my day of self-cultivation.

"You look funny, Mother."

"I don't think she does! Are you off your diet tonight?"

"Sky's the limit."

"I hope my husband doesn't mind about my weight."

"Your daddy never notices my weight."

"Then why are you always on a diet? And why won't you tell him how much you weigh?"

"I'm the one who cares. If he knew, he'd drop it in some casual conversation, and I don't want the whole world to know."

"I don't think you are fat, Mother."

"That's because I eat chocolate cake one time a year late at night with my son and daughter!"

They exchange the intimate look of conspirators. Karen asks, "Did Yana and Cheezy go to sleep?"

"Finally."

David says, "Cristen has nicknamed all of us, even herself." He helps himself to another piece of cake. "I wish Daddy could celebrate his birthday with us."

"Mother, tell us about the time Daddy took all of us to Clorinda."

"So! Late bedtime isn't enough! You scalawags want stories too!"

"Please!" Together they draw out the *e* sound.

I pour another cup of tea and look into eager faces that are smaller versions of the one in surgery now. With a long sigh, I lean back and so do they.

"You remember that Clorinda is a town in Argentina?"

They nod, eagerly helping me set the stage.

"But even though it is in Argentina, it is much closer to life here in Paraguay because it is far away from Buenos Aires and the busy life there. The pastor of the church in Clorinda asked Daddy to give a series of lectures on the Christian home one Mother's Day weekend. Naturally, he wanted us along as Exhibit A."

Karen interrupted. "If it were Mother's Day, why did they have a daddy do the lectures?"

David frowned. "Shhh! Don't mess up the story."

"They asked Daddy because I would not have dragged all of us over there! I should have sensed something in the low-hanging clouds or felt a warning in the passenger fare we had to pay for our suitcase on the bus downtown. Rain was falling by the time we reached the port. That should have signaled us to turn back. Leanne was a year and a half. She almost tumbled from the wharf into the bay. That certainly should have done it. But a package that carries a holiday and the honor of being an illustration was too great to forfeit.

"By the time the launch came for us, there was a steady downpour. A man from Clorinda who works in Asuncion had come to take the launch with us. It was Saturday afternoon, and things were already closed down for the weekend. The rain made everyone stay in who might have been out. Just our family and the man from Clorinda were passengers."

"We got to be friends, didn't we?"

"We certainly did! He was fascinated by Leanne's blond hair and blue eyes. He took her in his care. I took you, David, and Karen stayed by Daddy while he carried our bag and umbrella."

"I probably helped him," Karen says proudly.

"To reach Clorinda, the boat turned downriver, then back up another river to Port Elisa, which was just a mud bank landing. In sunny weather, oxcarts met passengers and carried them across a narrow neck of land to another river that is the boundary between Paraguay and Argentina. Port officials were there to let people cross the stream. The port closed on Saturday afternoon, which meant we paid half again as much to be allowed to cross."

"We went across in boats," the children say together.

"Boys rowed us across," I nod. "We were some sight, huddled in that boat under one umbrella in the downpour."

"Did it keep us dry?" asks David.

"We were all soaked! We kept huddling under the umbrella because it seemed like we should try something. The Argentine port officials lined up under their shelter and watched us. The nice man with us had found out where we were going and why. While we scrambled, slid, and slipped up the opposite bank, he stayed with us, carrying Leanne. He took us to a boarding house and Daddy went on to the church to tell them we had arrived and to find out the plans for the evening."

"And then!" They say in unison, eyes shining in anticipation.

"He came back with strange tidings of little joy! Not only was the program canceled but also the pastor was nine hundred miles south in Buenos Aires."

"Were you mad?" asks Karen.

"It was too late for that. We had to survive the night and try to get back to Asuncion the next day. The rain fell in torrents all night and sounded like Noah's flood on the sheet metal roof. The leaks in and around the bed made it feel that way too!"

"And there weren't enough beds," states Karen matter of factly.

"We had a double bed, which was more like three quarter size. Daddy, Leanne, and I slept in it. There was a little cot. We put one of you at each end."

"I . . . "

"Don't interrupt, David."

"You interrupted! I wanted to tell about when I went to the country with Daddy and Uncle Bill. We rode horses after we left the car and rode a long time."

"He did not, did he, Mother?"

"We rode a long time, and Daddy and Uncle Bill left me with some people, and they gave me their best *mandioca* and I slept in my sleeping bag and got a hundred and four flea bites!"

"David! What does that have to do with this? Mother!"

"I didn't have a bed then, either."

"We awoke refreshed, confident Daddy would be expected to preach in the morning service which would give some sense to the venture. We arrived at the church walking on mud highheels, wet again, and visited Sunday School. At the end of the hour, the Sunday School Director presented us and said that perhaps we had some word for them. Thinking he would be asked to preach at the worship service, Daddy just stood to say we were leaving on furlough soon and wanted to take the greetings of the church to the brothers and sisters in the States. There were smiles all around, and people nodded that we had their permission to do so."

"I remember that on furlough!" exclaims Karen. "Everytime one of you spoke, you said, 'We bring you greetings from the churches in Paraguay and Clorinda.'"

"It was kind of an inside message between Daddy and me."

"Didn't anybody ever wonder what Clorinda was?" asks David.

"If they did, they didn't ask us! I slipped into an anteroom to get Leanne settled for worship. In a few seconds, I heard everyone leaving. I opened the door and hissed to Daddy, 'What happened?' He said, 'He dismissed them! It's over!' I said, 'With you here and with the pastor gone, they dismissed? Didn't the pastor's wife tell him?' He answered, 'I guess not.'"

"Did we just leave, then?"

"We started trying. We picked up you children, the bag, and the umbrella, by then in tatters, and started the trek back to the river. We had to pay double to be ferried because it was Sunday, as opposed to fare and a half on Saturday afternoon. And the neck of land we had walked across was flooded, so we had to hire a boy with a canoe to take us around to Port Elisa. When we got there, we had the good word that the last launch for the day to Asuncion had left thirty minutes before we got there."

"Was it still raining?" asks Karen.

"Like Iguassu Falls."

"Was that when you told Daddy you were going to hit him?" David asks.

The three of us laugh. "Remember? It was Mother's Day. Everything I started to do, he would take over and say, 'Here, I'll do it, this is Mother's Day.' When we got to Port Elisa, he said that when I lifted the bag. It was then that I said, 'If you say it's Mother's Day one more time, I am going to hit you with this umbrella!'"

"Was that when we went up the Paraguay River in the little motorboat?" David wants to know.

"When we realized we had missed the launch, two young men and a boy began loosening a boat and offering to take us. I asked if their boat had a motor. I'd have stayed at Port Elisa before getting in a rowboat on the Paraguay in that rain. In we went, lurching forward, with one of our captains fore, the other, aft, and the boy bailing water in the middle. We had an oversized dish-towel-looking shelter stretched over us. The most memorable Mother's Day of my life was that one, as we hunched in our tiny boat in the middle of the mile-wide Paraguay River struggling against the current to reach port. When we went by the big Shell gasoline tanks, inch by inch, I nudged Daddy and told him if we ran out of gas, it would happen there in front of those storage tanks."

"And we got home." David ended the story.

"But Daddy is not the only one who gets into strange places," Karen said. "He didn't take the Girl Scouts on that field trip to see the ships. The place where the Paraguayan boats are sunk and in the sand."

"What can I say? You have two unusual parents. Besides, he went with us and kept the bull diverted while we ran down through the pasture to see what we could."

"I only saw a little bit of one," Karen says. "I don't understand how they got there."

"Riverbeds shift," I explain. "There was a lot of water when they went there. They were sunk in a battle."

"Did David know about the falls, or did I?" Karen wants to know.

"We discovered them together."

"I was so scared the day the wasps got Karen," David says.

"They didn't hurt so much. Daddy scared me the way he started hurrying us back to the hospital. But by the time we got to the lake and I was all right, he stopped for us to have tea on the hotel terrace."

"Mother, do we still have the picture of the lady with the cigar?" David asks. "Remember? She came to the falls one time when we were there with her water pot?"

"It's in the slide case," I respond.

"Don't talk about it, David! When Daddy asked if he could take her picture, I was so embarrassed."

I say, "He wanted her picture with that cigar."

"But then she smiled and spit it in the creek! He nearly broke his neck to get it and put back in her mouth!"

We begin to put our plates together. David says, "I will be glad when it's my birthday. Should I invite Dona Gilda to my friends party this year or to the family one?"

Karen has a solution. "Since your birthdays are on Thursday this year, have one on *senorita's* day."

"Would Aunt Wanda and Aunt Beverly and Aunt Ruth mind if we made it a party?"

"They would love it. Thursday lunch is sort of party time anyway. Gilda doesn't come every time, but we'll make sure she knows its a celebration for her and her twin."

We stack our dishes in the sink.

Karen asks, "Do you think Daddy might take us on another mobile clinic trip?"

"The last one was a disaster."

"Read us the article you wrote about it! Please!" They are together on the long *e* again.

"And the poems about it that you wrote for us!" they plead.

"Nope. You guys need to be in bed."

"Just this once." I'm a sucker for pleas by candlelight.

"OK. Then to bed. David, get the red notebook on my desk. I'll clear the table. Karen, turn on the light so I can read."

We sit again. I spread papers in front of my place and begin to read. "My surgeon husband and I are medical missionaries in Paraguay. As a doctor-nurse team we make periodic mobile clinic trips to the interior.

"He is devoted to togetherness and fearless of its consequences. On one of the clinic trips, he hoisted our three small children into the cab with fatherly pride. The remoteness of the town, the size of the truck's passenger area, and the ages of the children left me less than enthusiastic about that much togetherness. But with high resolve and fervent hearts, off we went to heal the afflicted.

"At the little church we held our clinic and worshiped with the brethren. Then the rain began—and continued. When we tried to drive the truck from the yard where it was parked, we stuck in the mud.

"While efforts continued to extricate the truck, I had to dig Child Number One from the pile of mud she was under from standing too close to the whirling back wheel. Child Number Two fell into the morass created by the togetherness of two neighboring cow chips in the falling rain while he was leaping between the two.

"Hours flowed into each other like the raindrops. Before the truck was free of mud, the clutch burned out. We left it. With help from our new friends, we crossed the swollen river in a darkness found only where the nearest electricity is fifty miles north.

"Refuge for the night was a dimly lighted rooming house. While the lady of the establishment was scampering about to prepare food, Child Number Three fell on the front porch and cut a gash in her left eyebrow. The laceration needed sutures, but all our equipment was securely locked in the truck in the black night across

the river. Wilbur fashioned several butterfly strips from the yellowed
adhesive tape he found on a shelf and closed the wound. After
wolfing down a modest meal, we fell exhausted into bed.

"Morning dawned like the first glorious one of creation.
Unfortunately, our appearance did not match the day. We saw
ourselves in wrinkled, dirty clothes, spotted with mud, manure, and
blood, stranded with a truck and three small children to get through
muddy back roads to the asphalt one and on home. We could have
cried, but survived by laughing.

"Our eventual release came by my walking with the little ones
twenty kilometers to the highway and hailing a bus that got us home
in the late afternoon. Wilbur returned with the clinic truck in the
middle of the night, towed by a lumber truck."

"Now the poems! Don't leave out the funny part," chortles
David.

"You mean the interpretations?"

He nods and rocks back and forth, wearing his teeth in a smile.

"Mobile Clinic Poetry, Command Performance!"
Building blocks for future glory,
Casting molds for memories,
Captured bits of fond remembering,
Forging today tomorrow's gold.
(Let's have togetherness! Let's take the
whole family on a mobile clinic trip!)
My debt, I find, is to all mankind,
Suffering, gasping, pleading, begging,
They wait just out my circle there,
Destitute, starving, all mankind.
(Those with headache, this line!
Those with worms, this line!
Those with backache, this line!)
Joy peals forth and echoes back,
Hoarse cries of victory from a hundred throats!
But wait! Joy now lies dead,

Murdered e'er she sprang full forth!
(The clinic is out of the mud, but the gears won't work!)

"Had enough?" I see eyes less awake.
"No! Keep reading."

Gaiety, laughter, running steps,
Calmness, stillness, shattered by screams,
Hysteria's cries rip wide the air,
Scarlet fountain, pale, pale skin.
(Leanne! I TOLD you to quit running.)
Patient, teaching, searching, reaching,
Eyes unblinking, watching, waiting,
Such newness here, unseen before,
Repeating still, repeating, still.
(Karen, they don't understand instructions on relativity.)
I did not think we'd end this way.
Our love is made of firmer stuff.
But such cruel things do come to pass,
And naught is left but tears of grief!
*(Honey, I hate to leave you with the clinic,
but I'm going to hike with the kids to the* ruta
and get a bus home.)

"Is that all?"
"Yes."
"Read them again."
"Not a chance. Off to bed, rascals!"
"Write another verse. We'll wait."
"Bed!"

They surrender and hug me goodnight. "We liked Daddy's party."

The tea I poured is cold. I heat more water and look in the refrigerator. A piece of cake is no substitute for dinner at the Guarani Hotel. Balancing a sandwich and fresh tea, I walk to the front porch and look three quarters of the way down the hill behind the church to see the surgery suite lights ablaze.

On an impulse, I get the cake from the kitchen and glide like a shadow down the hill. A white wrapped face answers my tap at the back door.

"Si?"

"Today is my husband's birthday. You all might like to celebrate when you finish the operation."

"Muchas gracias, senora." Arms covered in white fabric lift it through the door.

Wandering around the south side of the house, I make my way to "the swing," my special refuge in the backyard. I rock peace through all my spirit until sleep tugs hard.

In the bedroom, I stoop and pull from under my side of the bed my beautiful surprise and admire the ceramic chess set of medieval characters I made while on furlough. Hours were spent on them here, filling the pieces with plaster, staining, antiquing, polishing. Its beauty is enhanced by a chessboard made of inlaid woods from Brazil. In satisfaction I stare, then stick out my tongue at the queens sitting smugly by their kings.

With care, I take it to the living room, put it on the table nearest the door, turn on a lamp above it, and place a paper by it on which I have written, "Happy birthday! I love you."

"He'll be sleepy. Wouldn't want him to stumble over you." I move the table a bit to the side.

Approving the effect, I wink at the queens and go to bed.

7
In Missionary Support

"Our denomination has a three-pronged emphasis on missionary support," I say to Annie, my friend from another mission group in town. We were first-term missionaries together and have done a lot of mutual burden bearing for each other.

"Jenny, be careful," she calls to her little girl.

"Leanne, show her how to get from the edge into the wading pool," I say to my five-year-old. We sit in my yard and watch our children.

"Too bad Myrta couldn't stay," Annie says. "I wish they didn't have to spend so much time writing home to raise their support." We rock in the chairs and ponder the problems of another friend who is in the country without support from a funded board. "She types letters every day to lay their work before some group or explain how they used the money a church sent or to plead with some pastor not to drop them from the budget because there is a new program starting there."

"That doesn't leave her and her husband much time for what they came to do."

"Do Southern Baptists respond to the general emphasis without the kind of contact Myrta and her husband make?"

"It's a mixed reaction."

"Our people become impersonal about it, like paying a bill."

"Recently I read a letter to the editor of *The Commission,* our missions magazine, with an indirect slam at our program because churches don't know missionaries. So I wrote a letter to the editor about his letter to the editor."

"What did you say?"

"I started by extolling the missionaries who identify with the people they serve in foreign countries. I mentioned the War of the Triple Alliance and how that is still a divisive factor but that my sentiments lie, frankly, with Paraguay, though I certainly want all Argentines and Brazilians to know the Lord. My sympathies are with Paraguayans, my lot is cast with them, and what comes to them, comes to me. I tried the comparison of the emotion a pastor has for his flock. He would have respect and love for other churches, but his first devotion is to his own church."

"Sounds like that man's letter got you up in arms."

"It was the attack on missionaries, schools, seminaries, and the Foreign Mission Board. It was an assassination attempt on our mission-support system."

"He did that?"

"He talked about blind support of missionaries, not knowing them, subtly supported the individual church-missionary arrangement of faith missionaries."

"Faith!"

"That's why Myrta's situation reminded me of the brother."

"Did you make a response about faith missionaries?"

"I said the term makes me see red! I went on to say that it takes just as much faith for me to leave my home and loved ones, that the term relegates faith to a monetary value, implying that those who have less money have more faith than those who have more funds, and I closed that paragraph with a question."

"Which was?"

"Does the pastor of a big city church have less faith because he has a bigger salary than the pastor of a small or rural church?"

"You're going to hear from that!"

"It's kind of lost down in all the rest. I said that any Southern Baptist church can know any missionary. There are all sorts of pictures and data on record. Some missions-minded churches adopt missionaries and pay their salaries. But if new pastors or new church emphases come along not inclined to the practice, the board resumes the salaries so that a missionary is not left bereft."

"All of us enjoy that kind of personal contact with a church."

"I have never known a missionary who would not correspond with a church or individuals who have a desire to know him or her better. We all have furloughs, and we go to any church who invites us to share our ministry."

"Was that all you said?"

"I picked up on blind support, as he labeled it. Said I assumed that indicated dissatisfaction with the Cooperative Program and Lottie Moon Christmas Offering type of support as opposed to direct contact and described what we see here every day with Myrta and her family. They have to spend hour after hour in correspondence, drumming up their support so they can stay on the field. Precious time they would prefer to spend in missionary endeavors must be used in the task of writing, in a sense, begging for money. The system, to me, is not worthy of God's people or his work."

"I can't ask people to give me money."

"Nor I. But I can, with enthusiasm, present to God's people what their gifts have done in my area and help them see that this is multiplied many times around the world."

"I don't think anyone will answer your letter."

"I confronted the slap at missionary education. Said I considered the implication that we don't know the Bible to be an insult to every missionary who has gone through the rigorous study and appointment procedures of the Foreign Mission Board and at the personnel department who helps us along the process."

"Is that a typical attitude?"

"The truth is, Southern Baptists love missions and support the program with a great deal of trust and faith."

"What kinds of support do you receive?"

"Study, prayer, and giving. In turn, each stresses the intellectual, spiritual, and financial foundations of missions."

"Sounds good. Does it work?"

"The concepts are fantastic. Implementation breaks down in a few places."

"Like?"

"Take study, the intellectual base. I get the feeling that people at home don't quite make the connection between the places in missions periodicals and the same places that are in the evening news. Of course, when they don't know world situations or think about the reality of the missionary presence in a trouble spot or anywhere else, they only have a partial image of what is going on. They can't pray intelligently. Prayer effectiveness is blunted."

"Do you think people really pray for us out here?"

"Some do. I believe most of our people want to. They may not know how or what to pray."

"I recently wrote a prayer guide for our women. It was very difficult to do," Annie says.

"I have a hard time with that too," I admit. "You want prayer requests to be memorable, but you don't want to swamp people with so much they are overwhelmed."

"And it has to sound more specific and attainable than 'God save Paraguay.'"

"And it has to be ethical," I add. "A friend of ours told us about a missionary in another country who wrote a lot of letters home asking people to pray for God to open a way for a building to be built for his work when the Mission had voted to put it on a low-line priority."

"I hadn't thought of trying to manipulate God with prayer requests at home."

"And a friend in another country wrote a letter asking for prayer that missionaries be exempted from paying US income tax. In the same letter, he wanted prayer that some equipment being held in customs in his host country have the duty tax lifted."

"Are you Baptists having trouble with separation of church and state?"

"He just wanted the government subsidy on both ends. I don't think it even occurred to him what he was saying. He was going to help render to God that which Caesar didn't need."

"Missionaries aren't the only ones who get blurred vision about ethics in prayer."

"No! While we were on furlough, I sat in a meeting when a man gave a report on a visit he made to Paraguay while I was here! If I hadn't known his name and remembered his visit, I would never have recognized the hospital from his description. He meant well. The whole point of his message was to inspire prayer support. But the truth of the work is so much more inspirational than the stuff he fabricated."

"Why do people do that? Do they mean to be dishonest?"

"Seems to me we've spiritualized prayer and religious living to the point that, once we couch it in holy language, it becomes truth to us whether it is or not."

"Outdated prayer requests bother me."

"In what way?" I ask.

"When someone wants to make a point and a prayer request is used that is pertinent to that emphasis of the message, whether it is current or even still valid."

"I don't understand."

"I heard a sermon recently, here, that had a beautiful exposition of points about prayer, but the one on requests, neatly as it fit, happened six years ago."

"The open-ended requests trouble me. People are asked to pray about something and it is never mentioned again. I think missionaries need to keep the prayer requests to the States updated and to tell of answered prayers."

A flurry from the wading pool interrupts. Squeals split the air.

"Mommie! Princess jumped in the water!"

"Get her out."

"I can't!"

Walking to the children, I bend and lift a dripping cocker spaniel from between them.

"I'll put her on the other side of the fence." Brown liquid eyes chasten me as I carry her and drop her over the wire. I call back to Annie. "Do you want something to drink?"

"Thanks, no. We need to go soon."

"Let's move over to this shade."

We rearrange our chairs and watch our little ones. Annie breaks the silence. "I wish we could help Myrta in some way."

"So do I. I guess going to a mission field is a little like getting married. The future depends on the partner you choose. Linking with a denomination and a sending board certainly forms a commitment and a partnership."

"Do Southern Baptists respond to the missions information challenge?"

"Do you mean the emphasis on the study of missions?"

She nods.

"Woman's Missionary Union (WMU) puts out fantastic material. But it's not always used by the churches as well as it could be."

"Why is that?"

"I don't know, but I have a hunch."

"Which is?"

"Some of our churches still think of mission support as women's work. The teaching emphasis does not come through the strength of the total church program in a practical way. WMU and the financial aspect of mission support get center stage three times a year for the special offerings. But the week-by-week informational input doesn't get absorbed by the total church. The rest of the year it's an attitude of that being something the women do."

"But Southern Baptist money seems to hold up and keep coming."

"Our people love their mission work and missionaries. WMU and our two missionary boards do a great job with missions challenge. Convention leadership budgets financial support."

"But there is never enough."

"Never! In fact, we've just done a cost of living study."

"For what?"

"We do them periodically for the board to judge inflation for budget considerations for the work and salaries."

"Think you'll get an increase?"

"Nope. But they'll read the request carefully. I'm sending one of my songs with it."

"Maybe you should accompany the study and present it in person."

"We wouldn't have a prayer!"

8
In Marketplaces

The alarm clock screams. My hand automatically reaches out. Mists of sleep swirl, and I gradually emerge into consciousness. It is 5:00 AM and market day! I do a quick mental calculation. In about six weeks the weather will be cooler, and I won't have to go so early to beat the heat. Beat the heat, ha! I am already sweltering.

Swinging my feet to the floor, I look at my sleeping husband, sprawled in utter exhaustion. I remember the special evening we had planned last night. When he still hadn't returned from the hospital after a wait of an hour and twenty minutes, I took off my best black dress and went to bed. I have vague recollections of phone calls and emergency surgery during the night.

"Ah, Madame Medicine, you are indeed a jealous mistress, but I do always win eventually, you know."

I congratulate myself on being so philosophical—and remember many times when I haven't been. I reset the clock for 6:00 AM with a flourish and turn to the unconscious form.

"To you, my love, I give the priceless gift of another hour's sleep," I softly whisper.

I dress and brush my teeth, noticing, as I always do, that the water swirls down the drain the opposite direction in Paraguay. *Or maybe Oklahoma is off,* I muse. Past sleeping children, I slip quietly down the hall. In the kitchen, I leave preparations for a cold breakfast.

I unlock the garage, open the car, and put in four baskets. Remembering planned guests for the week, I make a quick guess as to the number of unplanned ones. I shrug and pitch in another basket. Backing out of the driveway, I think with materialistic longing of those marvelous brown paper bags in the supermarkets in the States.

I'm on my way. I see all that I've seen hundreds of times—crammed, dilapidated buses, street vendors, speeding cars—all that furor before 6:00 AM!

The colors are so intense I have to squint my eyes: blue, blue sky; green in plants; wild red and orange flowering trees.

"Ah, Paraguay, you are so gorgeous, and I love you! But you are so savage with your heat, your poverty, your suffering, and I hate you!"

Paraguay does not answer me.

And now, here I am at the market. I look out on the scene. Putting my head down on the steering wheel, I say, "Omnipotent God, Creator and Lord of the universe, let me see a frozen food case and savor the joy of double-stamp day just once more before I die."

With no spiritual surge assuring me I will, I sigh and get out.

And then the smells! Will I ever adjust to the mission field smells? I ask myself this question almost every day. Theologians may conjecture that Paul's thorn in the flesh was poor eyesight. From the first moment I set foot on a mission field I have never doubted that his thorn was a sensitive nose!

Here come the children.

"*Senora,* let me carry your basket!"

I hesitate. Is it right to deny them the few cents they can earn by carrying my baskets? I recall my own private crusade to teach them the dignity of work by carrying my own baskets. There have been times when I've triumphed in my private crusades—probably as many or more times when I've failed completely. But never have I quit in the middle of one.

"No, thank you," I smiled brightly, "I'll carry my own."

I start up the U-shaped passageway. The market women are on either side. Some have their wares on the ground. The more affluent ones have stalls. They all begin in unison, as if directed by some invisible conductor, calling to me to buy their bargains. After many years I have my regulars. I go first to the meat building. There is the Roast-Steak-Cutlet Woman. She greets me.

"Hola, Marchante."

"Hola, Marchante," I reply and wonder as I always do why we call each other *Marchante*. It undoubtedly comes from the verb *marchar* meaning to go forward, but beyond that I have no theories.

While she prepares my usual order, she says in a pouting voice, "You didn't come last week."

"No, I didn't."

"You must have bought meat somewhere else," she persists.

"Well, the truth is, *Senora,* I had a sick child; a friend bought a few things for me until I could come again. You mustn't be upset if I don't always get here on my usual day."

"Oh, no! I'm not upset," she breaks out in smiles. "I just want to be sure to have what you want when you come."

"I always like what you have," I assure her. I know she is not trying to be rude. This is the only way she knows to say she appreciates my buying from her. She is just reminding me that I belong to her. It's the market code. She empties the chunks of meat in my basket and puts a newspaper on top. I pay her, and we say good-bye.

I turn to the stall next to her to Don Tito, the Sausage-Hamburger-Pork Meat-Specialty Man.

"Buenos dias," he says with his slight, inclining bow and the partial smile that always begins on the right side of his face.

"Buenos dias," I reply and give him my order. While he is preparing it, I ask, "Don Tito, could you please change this bill for me? The fruit and vegetable women never have change."

He looks in his small wooden cash box. *"Senora,* I can't change it, but I will loan you this." He holds up several smaller bills. I do some quick adding. Only paper money and no coins always make me feel like I'm playing Monopoly when I go to the market. I decide his loan will just about get me around to the Potato-Tomato-Onion-Egg Man where I can get change.

"Thank you, so much. I will return it when I get change."

"*A sus ordenes,*" he smiles as he adds chunks of meat to a growing pile in my basket. He dismisses me with his slight bow. Courtliness is where one finds it.

I thread my way back to the car with my ten-to-twelve kilos of meat through groups of young women, obviously maids of the well-to-do, and others who are just shopping. They have the usual small bag or basket, buying bits of this and that. I marvel anew that anyone can placidly go to market every day and buy just that day's food without shaking a fist in the face of fate. Well, I'm just as strange to them, buying baskets and baskets of food once a week. But for the refrigerator and the freezer, there go I! Pleasure courses through me as I recall the security I feel when I sit in my kitchen and listen to the hum of my appliances. Materialistic? Maybe. But there isn't much time to develop the spirit when the work of all those lovely appliances must be done by hand.

I put the meat basket in the car and take out an empty basket. A little girl is back.

"*Senora,* may I carry your basket?"

"No, thank you," I smile.

I start for the Tangerine-Banana-Pineapple Woman—a regular. A woman stops me.

"*Senora,* do you want *mandioca?*"

"No, thank you. I bought from you the last time I was here. You gave me old *mandioca* and charged me double the price."

Utter shock! "*Senora,* how could that be?"

"Well, I'm not sure. I expect you thought I wouldn't know the difference," I say gently.

She looks down, to either side, and says in a hushed tone, "Buy from me today, and I will put in extra."

"Another time," I say, "I really don't need *mandioca* today."

We smile and part friends.

I carry out a basket of tangerines and return with an empty basket for bananas and pineapple. The *Marchante* and I chat while she fills my basket.

"How is your sister's new baby?" I ask.

"So pretty," she beams. "But my sister is not doing so well. She is with me now. Her husband went to Buenos Aires to look for work."

"Perhaps she needs medical attention," I venture.

"She does. She does. But we have so little money. And with her husband gone . . . " Her voice trails off.

"Bring her to our hospital," I say. "At the Baptist Hospital a person pays what he can afford to pay. If your sister has no money, she can still be treated."

There is relief in her eyes. "Maybe I will bring her."

We say good-bye. I head for the car. Halfway there, I hear a call. Ah! The Cornmeal *Marchante*—a regular.

"You are taking nothing from me today?"

"Oh, yes. I just wasn't thinking. The usual, a pound."

While she scoops the meal into the ubiquitous newspaper, I notice a woman by her side, obviously a friend. She smiles shyly and says, "I saw you Saturday night at the wedding."

"Really?" I ask. "Are you a Baptist?"

"No," she replies, "but both of us have been going to the church in Trinidad. Pastor Ortiz said we could all go to the wedding at the Ciudad Nueva Church. We had never seen an evangelical wedding."

"What did you think about it?"

They exchange glances. "The people were awfully noisy, but we liked the ceremony in Spanish and the things the pastor said about marriage and home."

I take my cornmeal and pay for it. "I'm glad to know you are attending at Trinidad. Maybe we will see each other at a meeting." We smile.

The next basket is destined for vegetables. While the Bean *Marchante*—another regular—counts out six, little fist-sized mountains of beans (to wrap in a newspaper), I notice a man near a back entrance.

"What is that man handing out over there?" I ask.

"Some kind of religious leaflet—I don't know exactly," she answers.

I look again and feed the details into my cranial computer to come up with a guess as to which religious group.

"What do you think about all the different religious groups?"

"Ah," she laughs, twisting the ends of my newspaper bean bag, "we Paraguans know how to wear many coats."

I smile, too, mulling over that one.

Now I am ready for the last empty basket. I go to the young Japanese men who sell onions, potatoes, tomatoes, and eggs. They are brothers, part of a Japanese colony who immigrated to Paraguay after the war. We exchange Spanish greetings in North American and Japanese accents. They know what I usually take. The oldest and youngest brothers fill my basket. The middle one comes closer, smiling, ready to practice his English.

"How-are-you?"

"Very well, thank you."

"It-is-very—warm!"

"But soon we will have cooler weather."

"You-will-go—to-your—country-soon?"

"Not soon. We are here four years and in our country one."

"What-does-your—husband(?)-husband-do?"

"He is a doctor in the Baptist Hospital in Villa Morra."

"Ah, yes-I-know-that-place. We-live-near-Villa-Morra."

"There is a Baptist church by the hospital. There is a very active group of young people. Perhaps you and your brothers can attend the services sometime."

"Thank-you. We-will-see."

My things are ready. I pay.

"You-will-come-again—yesterday?"

I smile. "Yes, I will come again."

Remembering Don Tito, I return to give him his money. I go to the car and load the last basket. I slump behind the wheel and wipe my brow, upper lip, and the back of my neck and decide to go home to get everyone off to work and school. I'll shop for staples later today. Looking out, I pursue a mental monologue.

Goodbye, my friends. I will see you next week. Those stateside supermarkets simply don't offer you any competition. Never in all my life has a meat counter indicated it missed me, nor has a butcher acted the gallant, nor has an aisle of canned fruit reached out tentatively for friendship, nor have the dairy case and staple aisle been receptive to invitations to church. I salute you!

I drive off in an aura of well-being. My meditation continues about my various friends from the many levels of society here: the general's wife whom I met while I was house hunting; the several charming, cultured doctors' wives I have met through my husband's profession; the publicity executive's wife I met because her little girl and mine became such close friends; the women I have met at my church; the seamstress who sews much better than I; my market friends.

I doubt that I could satisfy the statistics lovers with my contacts. While the "It-was-a-great-revival-though-there-were-not-many-visible-results" attitude is not very satisfying, neither do I completely trust those reports that make a trip to the bakery sound like a spiritual awakening. The dramatic experiences do come, but usually the stable converts are the results of someone nurturing their friendships.

I think of the usual stateside concept of a missionary. Funny! A missionary! Some may think I simply float out on the wings of the dawn and "mish." The hour is right, but the floating is nearer a sleepy stumble. And I "mish" just like they do—by simple contacts with ordinary people. I've never yet walked out to find people falling down around me, asking to be told about Jesus!

Frowning a bit as I turn into the sun for the last lap home, I continue. I'm a planter, mostly, I decide. Sometimes I get to harvest some fruits. I can recall two incidents when I've taken produce to market, but mostly I'm a planter. And I like being a planter. I like the easy give-and-take of simple friendship that drifts inevitably to the same goal that I, in earlier days, tried to accomplish with frenetic salesmanship. I like the comfort of my own personal, private crusades. If they succeed, fine. If they don't, no harm, no perforated ulcers.

I turn in my drive. My very own Beau Brummel is jauntily striding down to the gate to stamp out his day's quota of disease.

"Hi! Where've you been?" He asks with a knowing twinkle.

"To market! To market!" I reply and twinkle right back at him.

9
In Missionary Travel

Dear Young Marrieds,

How special you were to us while we were home on furlough! We have missed having a church group our age, but you have given us a bank account of good experiences to draw on for the next four years. Perhaps in turn I can share with you our getting away and some of the trip back to Paraguay.

We had false bravery around my mother's house the week before we left. Dad and Mother Lewis came over to see us off with my family. He took the group to Glen's for "the last supper."

With the pressure of all the preparations, I hadn't packed our bags and did that after everyone was gone, so I was up all night with the final things. Smart! At the airport the next morning, we got the preliminaries over, bags checked, and made lots of nervous, noncommittal conversation. The departure of the flight was announced. Can't remember how I got on the plane. I kept my sunglasses on and my eyes shut. Wilbur was telling the children to take a good last look at Oklahoma City. All I wanted was to jump off, but didn't. We finally arrived at the hotel in New Orleans, totally exhausted. The Skinners, our fellow missionaries and next-door neighbors in Asuncion, who were returning also, had been calling us. Our reunion with them was the bright spot of the day.

I lay down around six. Wilbur ordered dinner and woke me to eat. I fell back in bed, didn't even undress. I didn't hear another word until eight the next morning. Wilbur had put everybody to bed and gotten up with Cristen the next morning. If he'd been on sale, I would have bought a dozen!

Bill Skinner and Wilbur left Monday morning to check with the forwarding agent for all of our freight and the hospital's. Between us we are taking twenty-eight crates of hospital supplies. They had to get "in-transit" visas for Argentina so we won't have to undo all of it in Buenos Aires. The two Skinner boys went with them. Fran and her two girls went out to shop. I didn't want to budge from the room. Had breakfast and lunch sent to the room. Wilbur returned in early afternoon and took the three older children to swim. Cristen and I slept.

We boarded the *SS Del Norte* of the Delta Line to start to South America on Tuesday afternoon. I did a bit of last-minute dime store shopping that morning. Primarily, I just wanted to store up the atmosphere to remember.

The others had gone to dinner when we began to move out. I took Cristen on deck, and we told our wonderful homeland good-bye. Around one in the morning, we got to the mouth of the river and the Gulf of Mexico. The first swells of the ocean rolled and rolled with the power of the deep.

That first night I went to a private corner of the top deck to see the last lights of America and make my separation peace. We were completely at sea Wednesday morning. I took care of Cristen, watched out the porthole, and thought of the hymn, "There's a wideness in God's mercy,/Like the wideness of the sea." And it's wide!

Everything is a study in blue like something from Picasso's "Blue Period." The sky is lighter. The water is like permanent blue-black ink. The ship is gray blue. The only contrast is the white froth the boat makes slicing the water. It is quite lovely. With the remote, withdrawn quality, a quiet flows into me. I feel a buoyancy returning, and the poet in my soul sits a little straighter. I would not have thought that leaving this time would be harder than the first time, but it was. That first morning I thought about the ship, just a dot on this ocean, with me in it, plowing steadily on. I looked at little Cristen, so happy and secure just being with me, trusting me, and I found a parable for myself.

I went up on deck to see the stars and the sky. There is no blackness like a moonless night at sea, and the moon didn't come up until after midnight. In student days I aspired to be an astronomer. My love for the stars is hypnotic. They bring me a great sense of the presence of God. I made a ritual and liturgy of saying good-bye to the northern constellations and sat visiting with them for a long time. I lingered with the Dippers and Cassiopeia. Orion hunts south, too, so I won't lose him.

With some sleep, lazy eating, and fun with the Skinners, the leaving was left and adventure took its place.

You would probably be interested in what life for missionaries is like aboard ship—*Hawaii* notwithstanding!

Meals are served on this schedule: Breakfast—8:15-9:15; lunch—12:30-2:00 (in port) and 12:00-1:00 on the inside deck while at sea; dinner—6:30-8:00. In addition, there is coffee at mid-morning and tea at three in the afternoon. After ten at night, sandwiches are available on the inside deck. Our favorite psalm is "Bless the Lord, Oh, my soul: and all that is within me!"

We do other things than eat. We have taught the Skinners to play Yahtze. The four of us, playing until midnight, make more noise than anyone in the deck cafe area.

There are a number of young families with small children aboard; they don't stay up late. A few days ago one of the crew commented on what a sleepy bunch of passengers were on board. He went on to say that they took a boat full of missionaries not long ago who were a more swinging group than the present one!

Some interesting people are traveling with us. The brother of the Argentine consul in New Orleans is aboard with his family and mother and father. We taught him to play Yahtze too. One man is a department store executive from California on a vacation cruise with his family. A few are in private industry en route to Brazil.

The most interesting person is a retired rear admiral from the US Navy. He didn't like retirement and now has a law degree and teaches. He was King Neptune last night in the initiation ceremony and court for Pollywogs, those who had not crossed the equator before by ship. Leanne and Cristen are now Shellbacks with the rest of us.

The tournaments are in full swing: Ping-Pong, shuffleboard, all of it. Wilbur is still in the deck golf competition. We have movies at night and fire and boat drills once a week. One evening the special feature was bingo, and a bridge tournament is underway. We stick with Yahtze.

The steward watched Cristen for us the evening we were docked in San Juan, Puerto Rico. We put her to bed and took the other kids into town for a couple of hours. The old city is built around a square with forts on three sides to protect it. The wall is still in place. I could imagine Teddy Roosevelt charging up the hill. We slept in port and sailed the next morning.

The purser asked Wilbur and Bill to have church services during the trip. Last Sunday Bill presided and Wilbur preached. They will reverse roles next Sunday. Fran played the piano. I sat and looked like Julie Andrews!

In Bridgetown, Barbados, six of us went ashore. Calypso, I reckon! We saw small, picturesque things for a corner shelf in a collector's house. Karen, David, and I returned the next morning to look in the shops. Karen bought a doll for her collection and I got a spoon for mine.

One night we had a costume party. I made crepe paper outfits for David, Leanne, and Cristen. The rest of us used things we had. We went as Father and Mother Darling, Wendy, Tuffy, Peter Pan, and Tinker Bell. Leanne and Cristen were adorable—Peter Pan and Tinker Bell. As the latter, Cristen had big green balloons on her back and Wilbur carried her like she was flying. The judges awarded her first prize, which was totally honorary!

Rio was a treat this time! On our first trip, the weather was so murky we could not even see Sugar Loaf. We started into the harbor early in the morning and passed by the foot of Sugar Loaf Mountain a little after ten. We could see Corcovado, the peak to the south with

the huge statue of Christ on top, all of the time. We went to the top in
the afternoon. That was an adventure, like scaling a huge finger. It is
that steep. To reach the statue, there is additional climbing. The size
of the statue makes it grotesque up close. The view of the city and
the harbor from there is spectacular, but the 2,300 feet straight down
was a bit too much for this Oklahoma plainswoman.

We took in the palace of the former emperors, as well as the
great stadium, *Maracana,* where Billy Graham preached at the
meeting of the Baptist World Alliance. It is also where the
legendary Pele plays soccer. In spite of Rio traffic, we made it back
in time to sail with the ship.

The next port of call was Santos, port to Sao Paulo, the
industrial center of Brazil. Janice Skinner kept Cristen, and we took
the other three to the beach for the afternoon. It looked just like the
Copocabana in Rio with miles and miles of white beach and
skyscrapers going down to it.

David looked it over and said, "The trouble with the ocean is,
it comes up so close to the shore."

We found delightful little dressing areas on the beach but some
young men in a kind of uniform kept trying to tell us something.
Between their Portuguese and our Spanish we finally understood we
were not to dress in them. After a bit we also figured out the young
men were lifeguards.

Then they not only insisted we use their dressing areas but also
helped me wash the sand off the children and get them ready to
leave. After some hit-and-miss information, we took a bus back to
the ship. After an hour, we arrived and climbed aboard our floating
home.

The next stop is the last one, Buenos Aires. We hope we won't
need more than a couple of days there to get our things headed
upriver. The plan this time is for the people to fly! By Wednesday we
should be home. We are eager!

This unstructured travelogue is my attempt to share this aspect
of our world with you there because of all you shared with us in

every gesture and deed that spoke of your care and love. We love you and will cherish all we have known together the past several months.

My love and affection,
Gladys

Dear Family,

You had notes and cards from me as we passed through ports on the way down. I wrote you last in Sao Paulo.

One more hop and we were in Buenos Aires, the end of our voyage by ship. I hated for it to be over, in a sense. Having to pack again influenced my feelings!

Missionary friends met us. They had hired a dispatcher to clear our baggage. Fran Skinner and I and the children went on to the seminary and to the home of friends for supper. Wilbur and Bill stayed to clear our hand baggage. None of the traumatic things that happened our first time through occurred this time.

All the details were cleared by Wednesday. We were able to get the flight we wanted and sent a telegram to our Mission in Paraguay on Monday morning telling them we would be arriving. But in true Latin fashion, Monday and Tuesday were holidays. The telegram was not delivered. No one was at the airport to meet us and bring us home. You will remember that, by a similar comedy of errors, no one met us the first time we came. The Skinners say they aren't going to travel with us anymore. There was a real shock wave around the hospital when Bill called to announce the arrival of the Skinners and the Lewises. We had a joyous reunion when people did come crowding out to the airport.

The flight from Buenos Aires to Asuncion lasted an hour and a half. The first time we were on the riverboat six days. I looked down on the snaking river and thumbed my nose at it.

There have been a lot of changes, but my first impressions hit me hard! As we were landing, I turned to Bill and Glen Skinner behind me and said, "Wow, it's worse than I remembered!"

At that second, Glen was saying, "It surely has changed." Bill guffawed. He said we were saying the same thing, but Glen was being more diplomatic.

As we unloaded and walked up to the front of the hospital, a man drove up to deliver the telegram we sent on Monday to tell our arrival time. Ah, Paraguay! Here I am, my beloved, back with you, where the chickens start crowing at ten thirty at night and nothing ever goes according to plan or schedule!

It's a relief, in a way.

I will be back in touch as we get settled.

We love you. The separation from you is dreadful, and scarcely a day goes by when I don't think of you and wish we could do this without the absence.

FROM YOUR SOUTHERN FAMILY,
GLADYS

10
In Furlough

Three empty trunks, battered by the trip from furlough, are stacked in the corner. Barrels stand around me on the porch, mute sentinels, guarding the door from my escape.

"Mother, will you unpack the barrel today that has our toys?" comes the polite request from my ten-year-old.

"I want my racetrack!" is the less polite statement from the eight-year-old.

"Toys!" yells the four-year-old.

My ten-month-old baby sits placidly in the jump seat, chews Mickey Mouse's right ear, and surveys the scene.

"One thing about heaven, I won't have to pack barrels to go," I mumble.

"What did you say, Mother?"

"I said, 'Good heavens, I need to get to work on these barrels.'"

"May we help?"

"Let's push this dolly over here by the barrel. When I lift the edge of the barrel, you push the shelf edge of the dolly under it. We'll roll it to my bedroom and open it."

"Is my racetrack in that one?"

"This one has all the toys and a few odds and ends."

In the bedroom, I unlock the band and lift it from the top. With the top off and leaning against the wall, excitement mounts.

"Do you see my racetrack?"

We lift games, dolls, books, and finally the racetrack into boxes.

"How about the three of you taking these boxes to the playroom and putting your things in place?"

The babble moves down the hall. I hear the pecking order established and functioning.

"You may have these shelves. You take these. I will put my things here," Karen instructs.

"Your shelf is wider," complains David.

"So are my books," concludes Karen.

"My toys?" asks Leanne.

"Right there."

I turn to the barrel and the baby watching it and me. Her attention is now on Mickey Mouse's other ear.

"Missy, let's get the rest of this out."

She smiles around Mickey's ear.

I bend over the barrel and pull out handfuls of things. Pitching them on the bed, I begin to sort them. I have tried other ways to pack, but the metal drums are for me the most efficient and offer the most protection. I fold a white pima cotton shirt my sister gave me for Christmas. My favorite, I wore it to the last, then stuck it in this barrel. Memories of the last few days stateside crowd in on me.

The main sacrifice of missionary living is separation from family. Grandparents had not seen Karen and David for four years, and Leanne, not at all. Cristen was born during furlough, but she will be nearly five by the time they see her again. We crammed a lot into the time with them, made up for the years we were gone as much as we could, and stored a bit for the future.

Before going on furlough, Karen and David were with me going to the market one day. She was instructing him in the American way.

"You don't remember the States."

"I do too!"

Undaunted. "You probably don't remember Granny either. She's so nice. She'll buy you anything you want!" This from the little one who said before we left for overseas the first time, "Granny, I don't think you should give Mother and Daddy any money. They could get a job and work if they wanted to."

I pick up the Braniff flight wings pin the stewardess gave one of the children when we were going home. Nobody wants it anymore. I decide to keep it for myself. Braniff has two flights a week to the US. The flight pattern is near enough to our house that I can see the big bird as it begins its ascent through Paraguayan air space. Last term it became a symbol of otherness.

In the early days, when I was so homesick and unbelieving in the validity of my calling, it helped to go in the yard and watch the Braniff plane descend to the airport west of us. It made me feel less abandoned and bereft. If all else failed, I could get on that jet and reclaim my other life. It became a spiritual symbol of God and home.

With time those feelings faded and Braniff came to be the vehicle for bringing others to us to share in our work and world. The big adventure was to go to the airport to welcome a visitor or see some of the Mission family off or welcome some of us home.

"If I need the Braniff therapy, I shall wear my little wings while I watch." The source of Mickey's torture kicks in glee. I place the tin wings in my jewelry case.

Pushing aside some papers, I pick up the drama masks that hung in our dining area in the States during the furlough. I reach inside the fat, smiling face and pull out a tissue wrapped package. Slowly unwinding the paper, I see that the vial of Oklahoma dirt which I took from the backyard is still capped firmly with nothing spilled. I set it on the dresser.

"I shall put that by the fireplace," I announce to the baby. She smiles around Mickey's nose.

The masks were a gift I gave myself. On our first trip to Okmulgee to visit the Lewis grandparents, we went on to Sapulpa to a factory that sells slightly flawed and perfect dishes and other items. After choosing the dishes we needed, I saw the masks. They were on the display floor, full price, not seconds.

I said to Wilbur, "They look like us. I am the fat, laughing one. You are the skinny, sad one."

He gave them his full attention, then said, "They both look like you," and walked off to pay for our purchases. I stayed in front of the masks.

"He's right," I told the pottery faces. "I intensely love and hate, simultaneously." I picked them up with loving hands and walked to the wrapping desk.

"I have a check coming for those devotionals I wrote last month. I'm going to buy these."

"I'll buy them for you."

"Please. It's important I pay for them with money I earned."

He gave me a long look. "All right." He wrote the price of the masks on a piece of paper and handed it to me. "See that you pay your IOU."

I took them to the house our home church, First Baptist in Midwest City, provided for us those furlough months.

"I'm sure you've named them," Wilbur said one day.

"Adam and Eve."

"Which is which?"

"Depends on the mood they are in. Today Adam is the fat, happy one. Last week he was sad."

"I can tell there is a parable."

"The masks are humanity. If you feel intense pain, you can feel a correspondingly intense joy. You know, soar with eagles or walk. It's the rebound law. You can swing as high as you can fall."

"I've never heard of the rebound law."

"I just made it up."

"Figures."

"So now I must find an appropriate place for you." I finger the baked clay features. "What I really need to do is find a spot on the living room wall where I can see you through the window when I wear my wings and watch the Braniff jet fly over!"

Raised voices clamor from the playroom. As I listen, Big Sister brings order to chaos.

"Too bad God didn't have her on hand for the creation," I say to the cherub. "He could have pulled it off in five days and rested two!" Cherub kicks her legs and pats Mickey.

I pick up a fist of papers and something flutters to the floor.

"Will you look at this! I may have to thumbtack it next to Adam and Eve. A grocery list is all I need to start a memorial shrine to that great American knack for concentrated shopping in one place."

Cherub squeals her approval.

"If I could have paid our utility bills at the supermarket, I really would have had it all in one place."

I run an eye down the paper.

"Bet I ate apples and iceberg lettuce every day for two months, Missy."

Cherub jumps and throws Mickey on the floor. I bend to get the toy for her.

"You don't know my apple story." I kiss the top of her head. She gurgles and looks at me with wide eyes and half of Mickey in her mouth.

Opening a drawer, I get a nail file and sit on the floor in front of her to repair a snagging thumbnail.

"We had been here about three months. I went to the market one day and saw between the brown peas and the brown mandioca a small basket of gorgeous red apples. Walked by them three times before I decided to buy *one* because they were so expensive."

She springs in her seat, eager at my voice.

"I brought it home and took it straight to the bedroom to hide it in a drawer." I bite a loose cuticle at the edge of the nail. "Daddy came home, walked in the hall, and shot back in the kitchen. 'I smell apple,' he whispered. I took it from its hiding place that night, and we went outside to eat it so no one would hear or smell it. Most wonderful apple I ever had!"

She squeals and bangs Mickey on the tray of the jump seat. I pick her up and hug her. "Gave me a new slant on that Genesis story. Bet you Eden was right here in Paraguay! I know one thing. Could have led your daddy down any path with just the odor of that apple. Matter of fact, anybody could have led me almost anywhere the same way!"

Chubby arms hug me. "Nap time for you, Love. You have been nice today. Some days you wake up needing a nap." I carry her to her crib and return to the papers.

The one on top is a program from a WMU enlistment tea. I don't know why I kept it. Forgetting was my intention. David came down with scarlatina, and I called the hostess to tell her I couldn't be there to speak. She was so upset and worried about the program that I finally called my sweet mother to stay with the children. I put all of them, including David, in the car, went for her, brought them home, then went to speak at the tea. I drop the paper in a waste basket and stare at it. That one ranks with the trip to western Oklahoma to the day camp.

Six weeks before Cristen was born, I traveled across half the state with my little children, eight, six, two. We did our thing and, after a suitable wait, returned home. Those who invited us didn't offer to pay for our gasoline or even share food with my children.

Money has never caused me to do something I did not want to do, nor has the lack of it prevented my doing something I wanted to do. But there was not even a thank you. It was a graceless event, and I pondered it all the way home. That night I leaned back in a chair, put my swollen feet and legs on the huge basket of laundry I had left undone, and stared at them. I began laughing aloud.

David looked up from his cars on the floor. "What's funny, Mother?"

"I was thinking of a Bible verse."

"Bible verses are funny?"

"This one is. Isaiah 52:7 goes something like this, 'How beautiful upon the mountains are the feet of them that bring good tidings, that publish peace, that publish salvation.'"

I bend, take the program from the wastebasket, and move to the green chair by the window. Turning the paper in my hands I decide to keep it as an inverse memorial to all the wonderful things people have done for us. These two out of how many hundreds? In neither did anyone set out to be malicious. It was just unthinking insensitivity, probably brought on by the pressure of the responsibility of the task given. I'll keep it, fold it, and put it in the jewelry case by the wings.

Deputation speaking for a furloughing missionary is the ultimate in respect and adulation. How often the past months did I feel like the missionary child who said he wanted to be a missionary on furlough when he grew up!

Some people are in awe of missions and missionaries. If there is some insensitivity on the part of people to a missionary's situation, it is balanced by the temptation for the missionary to exploit the hero worship that Baptist people have for him or her.

The great trap in speaking about missions is to substitute the telling for the deed. A missionary hits on a story from his work. He tells it and, with the reaction of the people to it, the telling soon becomes more exciting than the doing was. His emotional action is vested in the stateside telling, not the foreign doing. It's hard not to exploit that because Baptist people want victory stories from their heroes.

I tried to accent the routineness of missionary life, but somehow it seemed to come off making me sound more humble than I am, with folks protesting my modesty.

If we have a good story, we ought to tell it. But the bad ones ought to be told once in awhile too. I always feel a tension between the realistic rendition of my authentic work, which is sometimes boring and my skill as a performer. I know my ability and performance as a speaker make me sought after, not the fact that I am a good missionary. I keep faith with my ethics, but the existence of the tension troubles me.

Once I began a speaking assignment with what happened to me the first time my name appeared on the birthday calendar. "My first birthday on the mission field, when thousands of Southern Baptists across our nation saw my name on the prayer calendar and prayed for me, was one of the worst experiences I can remember. Before ten o'clock that morning I had burned the entire back of my right hand, had a fight with my husband, been cheated out of six dollars at the market, and had a flat tire.

"By noon I had spanked both my children and broken a typewriter part which had to be ordered from the States.

"Between noon and two in the afternoon, it began to rain, so the laundry could not be hung outside. In an attempt to dry the clothes, a kerosene heater was lighted which smoked and blacked them.

"Before three a woman selling live chickens at my gate fussed at me for not buying one.

"At four the mechanic came to tell me the tire could not be fixed and that he would need some more time to buy another one and that maybe I could have the car *manana*. That meant I could not get to the next town to my church meeting at four thirty.

"I made sandwiches, put them on the table, took a sheet of paper, wrote on it 'Do Not Disturb,' taped it to the bedroom door, closed myself in, sat in a chair, and stared at the trees until dark."

The effect of that speech was the reverse of what I wanted. I loved having my name on the prayer calendar. Maybe somewhere down the line there'll be a miracle from it for me. Most of the time I need coping strength instead of miracles. But with my wild story, people didn't see the parallel between their lives and mine. I became more spiritual, more apart.

I went back to the entertaining stories. True—but highly entertaining.

Deputation speaking's real contribution is actually in the personal dimension. It puts personality, human life, in an impersonal entity, the Cooperative Program. Personal interaction is the real value.

After three months of meticulously explaining about Paraguay and having people say things afterward that let me know they thought it was near China or Israel and that I worked with Jane Doe in Hong Kong, I realized that information is not the issue. Personal interaction is the key.

I am at peace now knowing that people won't remember what I said, how I said it, or where I work.

But they will always remember me. Five years from now I can

meet them in a mall or they will see my name on the prayer calendar, and they will say to a friend that they know me.

"I saw and heard her at First Baptist Church! [Or Bethel, or Temple, or Immanuel, or. . . .] She's a missionary, you know. We support her and her family with the Lottie Moon Christmas Offering and the Cooperative Program."

That's the bottom line. And really, it's enough.

The last thing in the barrel is a crushed hat from Six Flags Over Texas. I take it to the playroom where Big Sister has organized the troops, and they are playing school.

She is giving a diction lesson to Leanne who has her own language.

"Say pat-*tern*."

"Pat-ter-ren."

"Sat-*chel*."

"Sat-*cher*-el."

Her word complexes and groups have made problems for family talk. She never got straight that the name of her favorite show was *Beverly Hillbillies* and not "Heavenly Beer Bellies" or to call footed pajamas anything but "hanger britches" since they hung there on her feet. She combined zippers and snaps into "snips," and the New Testament became the "New Intestine." We did what was done with David's "hopla-kopter" for applicator. We say it the way she does.

"Mother! Make her say it right."

"Have you forgotten 'ucky-bucky'?"

"I made up *new* words. She's messing up good ones."

I jam the hat on David's head. "I found your hat."

"Will we go on furlough again soon?" He looks at me with shining eyes.

"The time will be here sooner than we expect."

"I don't want to go," says Karen.

Sitting by her, I give her a hug.

"You will when it's time. We all will."

11
With Letters Home

DEAR FAMILY,

The house is being repainted, so we are in an unbearable mess. We have been unpacking the things we left stored. The smell of something that has been packed a year in this humidity is a challenge to your commitment to conservation. I would prefer to throw it all away.

We piled everything into the bedrooms while the front was painted, now have moved it all to the front to paint the bedrooms. There had been a drouth for months, but, of course, when they started painting, the rains came. This slowed matters because of a problem with the paint drying.

If I can leave while work is going on in the house, everyone benefits. The methods grate on my Anglo-Saxon compulsive efficiency. Scooping sand out of the flower beds to make a mud mixture to repair holes in the walls leaves me with my adrenals aquiver. They put a plaster over it and paint, but all of us feel better if I don't see it being done.

It's also better if I don't see how it's being done. A couple of men were helping me move some furniture. They came to me with wide eyes to announce a terrible problem.

"*Senora,* the door is too narrow," said one.

"Yes, and the chair is too wide," said the other.

"What do you mean?"

"The chair cannot be brought into the room where you wanted it." Man One.

"Because it won't go through the door," Man Two.

"Of course, it will pass through," I told them and went with them. They showed me with great happiness how they were right and I was wrong as they pushed the chair upright against the doorjamb.

"Turn it on its side like this, and turn it through the door like this."

When I passed by ten minutes later, they were still discussing the intelligence of *la senora*! I could tell them how to get it through but would be helpless if I broke its leg.

In the middle of the painting, a man brought by an orchid plant with five little branches that had fifty-two blossoms about two by three inches each and wanted to sell it for a little less than four dollars. I bought myself a welcome home present. The same afternoon an employee from the hospital brought me a smaller one with nine blossoms.

Latins farther south have discovered Paraguay as a Florida to escape their cold. All the hotels are full of tourists.

We are told this has helped the standard of living for some. But the first week we were home a woman came to the gate. It was raining. She had a small child in her arms and a large sheetlike cloth wrapped around them both. She asked for some food and clothes. When she did I could see most of her teeth were missing, not pulled, just rotted off at the gums. Everything is very disorganized, but I managed to find her a few things. She came again and the third time brought me some tomatoes and asked for more clothes. She had brought a friend with her who wanted some clothes too. They both obviously needed them. But I knew I couldn't go on with her because I would soon have a larger clientele than I could handle. I have some more clothes to give away but brought the majority for the people in our churches. I told her I didn't have anymore clothes to give her but would buy her tomatoes. I always feel bad in these situations. That night I didn't sleep well. Guess I will never adjust to being one of the haves in a world of have-nots.

New things are everywhere though. Some are funny. For example, a law was passed that the bread had to be covered. All of us buy our bread at a certain bakery. When I went the first time I saw them in their lovely new building with very nice glass-covered cabinets. The bread was either on top of the cabinets with flies crawling on it or in the cabinets with the flies closed in with it.

They had bought a new freezer! But it was setting in the middle of the floor. The next time I went it was in the same place. I asked the daughter of the owner where they were going to put it. She answered that they would probably leave it where it was because they had no room for it.

I looked around and said, "If you would pull those cabinets toward me, turn them to an *L,* you could put it on that wall."

She gave me some look. I came to help.

Karen's been a little unsettled by things not being just as she remembered. She said, "Well, I hope our church hasn't improved!"

Our drivers' licenses expired while we were gone. We sent the old ones to be renewed. The hospital driver came back to say that they had passed a new law while we were gone and that we would have to take the new written and driving test.

"Don't worry," he said, "it's just like they do in the United States."

We went one morning because the tests are only given at certain times. The man said we should return the next day to get the results, which we did. We passed the written part but were told we would have to come back in the afternoon for the driving test. After a long wait, we had the test in downtown Asuncion in the middle of that crazy traffic. Then we took all the papers to another office to pay and get the licenses. We had the written tests, papers for the driving tests, another paper we had to buy to get permission to take the test—bought from another office—with two special stamps on it bought from still another office.

The official checked our papers and asked Wilbur, "Where are your eye and ear examinations?"

In unison, we said, "Our what?"

The first office of the day before had neglected to tell us that we had to go to a special place for eye and ear exams. In going back to learn where, we discovered those exams could only be done in the mornings. At that moment up walked a dear friend and member of our church who works down there. He talked the clerk into letting us go to a private doctor for them.

"It must be an eye specialist," she admonished us.

We spent the next hour looking for the office of the eye doctor who comes to our hospital on consultations two afternoons a week. He had moved his office while we were gone.

When we found it, Wilbur gave the receptionist his card to give the doctor with the message of our need. She got everything right, except for telling him we were patients whom Wilbur was referring. We sat there an hour and a half.

With his paper, we hurried back to the first office fifteen minutes before closing time. They said they had already locked up their money and we would have to return the next day. Our friend appeared again and talked them into taking our money and a growing stack of papers. They agreed to do it if we had the exact change, which we did. But then they discovered they had not told us we had to have a picture made.

Back with the pictures I went the next day to get the licenses. I was told to take them to another office to have them laminated.

As I drove home with the two shiny new licenses, I mumbled to myself, "Just like in the United States!"

Now that we are beginning to put our household back together I have thought with a start how important it is to have something to say, "This is mine." I have things out, cleaned, and remembered associations with them of pleasant things that have happened. I wondered how Jesus felt about going home. I wonder if he had something kin to a favorite chair which brought special pleasure upon seeing it again.

I don't really want you to know how hard it was for me to leave you. I love you all so much. The time there was a gift of God. But in my sadness at leaving you, he also gives a joy at being again with these people. You would love them too. I hope someday you can come to visit and meet all the members of our other families.

The work in the hospital seems to be humming. We can't wait to be back in the thick of it. The churches are in a time of growth too. We sense a spirit of excitement. We are probably going to start a new church this term as a mission of the church where we were last term. I am eager about that, but a little scared too.

WE LOVE YOU,
GLADYS

DEAR PREACHER,
You keep popping in my mind today. Guess my camel's hump of stored English inspiration is beginning to get low. If I were there, you could preach me one of your good sermons and I'd be full and wonderful again!

We are so involved it hardly seems possible we ever left. One prevention of drowning is to stay out of water over your head, but the water was that high when we got off the plane. Even with all that goes on, I feel an absence of the tension that ate and slept with me while we were there. Can't quite put my finger on the reason why. It's a combination of things. I don't feel as though I have set the kingdom back five years if every little thing doesn't click according to plan. If I really reach an overload point, I can drop something and no one would question my devotion to God. I never have quit in the middle of a job, you understand, knowing my penchant for overkill! But I know I could.

This is not to say we don't have frustrations and coping loads. A few times I have gone in the back bedroom by myself and given Paraguay a good blistering with the aid of a few words I learned at my father's knee, then settled it up with a few from the Father. The reason I can stay is the hate and love balance with laughter as the fulcrum.

I distrust missionaries, or anyone, who are all sweetness and light. They are like that Dickens character, Uriah Heep. They also don't quite ring true. I have the same problem with devotional books, which Wilbur can't understand. I do not need inspiration for holy thoughts and loving deeds. I have more work than I can ever do and enough stuff in my head at any given moment for a legitimate headache. If anybody ever comes out with something on the-maintenance-of-pure-testimony-when-a-quart-of-milk-is-spilled-on-a-just-scrubbed-floor, I'd be willing to consider the purchase price.

Wish you could share our thrill at the growth of the churches. Ours quadrupled while we were gone. (I sound like a *Baptist Messenger* report, don't I?) We are now missionaries of the church in Fernando, as well as yours, for we have gone off to "mish" on our own. It is going well, but gets scary being number one on the firing line.

The adult Sunday School teacher in the Fernando church is a young lawyer, mayor of the town. He decided to take a census and named a committee of community leaders to do so: a teacher; our pastor, Elias; a priest; and a couple of others. You can imagine the prestige that gave our church, as well as an acceptance for Elias from the townspeople. He and the priest became very friendly. When Elias and Blasida had their wedding anniversary, Elias went to the priest's house to invite him to dinner with them. He accepted. In his church, he told his people they could come to our church if they wished and could send their children to our school if they wished. We now have a kindergarten and first grade that meet in the building during the week.

He said, "Some of our people will go there, but we'll get some of their people. We're not going to fight anymore."

I didn't have any great message to deliver or burden to share. You are my stateside English pastor/sermon symbol, and that's a very important person for somebody like me. I just wanted to touch on paper.

ONE OF YOUR SHEEP ON DUTY FOR THE FOLD,
GLAD

DEAR PHYLLIS,

Your letters are bits of cheesecake and applesauce, they are so special.

You're right, the whirl continues. There is one new slant since I

last wrote to you. I am a Girl Scout leader! I have agreed to try a
troop down here. There are twenty little girls, ranging from the US
ambassador's daughter, the daughter of the head of USAid, the US
Military Mission, and a few high-ranking Paraguayans, to the little
ones of all the missionary groups. I probably would not have much
contact with most of those people ordinarily. Here I am, cozy and
intimate as can be. I particularly enjoy the ambassador's wife and
the wife of the first secretary. Karen and Susan, daughter of the first
secretary and Karen's very close friend, have been invited to the
ambassador's residence several times to play with Crissi, the
ambassador's daughter. The three spent one interesting afternoon
riding up and down in the dumbwaiter at the residence and put it out
of order. I was humiliated. They explored all the residence, so I had
a first-hand report on the parts I had not seen.

These Scout-origin friendships are very important to me. In
addition to the enjoyment we mothers get from each other, there is a
contact with America there that we missionaries by ourselves can't
supply for each other. Parents' Night is such fun. We have badge
presentation every couple of months. The girls are so enthusiastic,
and they work on badge requirements a lot since there aren't as
many diversions for children here. One of the fathers flies to Panama
about every two weeks, so he buys the badges for me. The
International Zone has a Scout facility. Last Parents' Night we
presented, with all the other official things, an operetta of The Three
Little Pigs. It was part of a troop badge project. I wrote the script,
and the girls sang the parts in operatic voices to music they made up
as they sang. I made paper masks for them, and they made the
props. It was adorable. I was the most enthusiastic parent there! We
do these productions in my living room with the furniture out of the
living room and dining room, having seating as a theater for the
parents, we use the dinette area, at the end of the dining room, as
our stage. I do great with meetings and badge work, but when it
comes to outdoor life I am lost. When we are due an outing, I plan it
so that Wilbur, that old gung ho Scout of yesteryear can go along.
We borrow Wanda's VW van to take them on the trips.

I wrote my mother that you would call and borrow the tape we sent. Each of us, even Leanne and Cristen, recorded some things for all of you.

THANKS FOR WRITING—AND FOR FRIENDSHIP,

MY LOVE

P. S. I went to a lunch party for *Las Amigas,* the organization of North American women in the country last week. Sat with a woman who told me in great detail all through the meal how I looked exactly like someone in Brazil whom she had literally despised! Does that remind you of Barbara W.? What's with this face of mine! I finally said to her, "I wish you knew me better. It might make you feel better toward the woman in Brazil."

Mrs. Jeffrey Miller
WMU Director
Immanuel Baptist Church
Willoughby, Oklahoma

DEAR MRS. MILLER,

Your letter came the same day the notice came from the customs house advising me that a package had arrived for me from the States.

It was good for me to have your news and to sense the excitement of your group for missions. It was especially inspiring to learn of all the activities you have planned about you in your area. Missions connects locally, as well as with what is done here where I live. You are to be commended for the positive leadership you so evidently display. I feel certain your example is a model for missions in your church. I personally thank you for that.

I am glad that my article in *Royal Service* elicited from you and your organization a desire to do something tangible for our work here. I have reread it and can understand how it made you think of the things you sent in the package.

We had a bit of a delay in getting the package out of customs but do have it now. We were not able to use the tray cards at the hospital until last week. I enlisted the help of the children in Vacation Bible School where I worked week before last in copying the Spanish versions of the Bible verses beneath the ones you had written in English.

I have divided the dish towels between the hospital and our camp kitchen.

The big red scrapbook was lovely. The customs official especially liked it as red is the color of the dominant political party here. He mentioned several times, while I was waiting for him to check through the things, that he wished his son could have one like it. I didn't think you would mind if I gave it to him. I have read through some of the recipes you and the ladies clipped. They look yummy! There are a couple of substitutions I will need to make for the foods we can't get here. Our dietitian is going to translate them and put them in the hospital kitchen recipes.

Mrs. Miller, I do remember meeting you at Glorieta. We were together in the registration line during WMU Week. You had on a lovely powder blue pantsuit. I could associate you with Willoughby because a school friend once pastored Bethel Baptist Church there. His name is Hugh Bickers. His wife, Mary Sue, was my roommate the semester before they were married.

We always appreciate your interest. Please pray for us and our work. Continue to urge financial support of missions through the Foreign Mission Board. WMU has always played such an important part in missions education and information in the churches. It is my frank opinion that missions would not be what it is today without the sacrificial service of Southern Baptist women in WMU through the years.

YOUR FRIEND AND SISTER IN THE LORD,
GLADYS LEWIS

DEAR FAMILY,

With people off to school for the day, I have a good hour to get in a visit with you.

The children are still in the Asuncion Christian Academy, the cooperative school effort here. Karen has started seventh grade. She has an excellent teacher, a Mennonite man from Canada here for a couple of years. He is very good with science, which she has always loved, and told me he has her doing ninth grade work.

David has turned out to be a good student, too, which is a good feeling when I recall how I thought he'd never learn which was red, blue, and yellow when I was teaching him kindergarten. He is a writer! His teacher, a Mennonite lady from Oklahoma, no less, gives original composition and poetry assignments, using spelling words as a basis. He has been getting the first place vote of the class. This is without prize, of course, just a motivational thing. He loves sports, and some new North Americans have started a Saturday program of baseball and soccer. We have given him judo lessons for his birthday at an academy between here and the church.

Leanne has the first grade in hand. She did something none of the others have done. Her first grade card had straight tens, which equivalent to A's. It was good to have an indicator from her. I am not good at assessing their performance. They all seem brilliant to me.

Cristen calls the shots now. A couple of weeks ago I took David to the barbershop and would not let her go with us. She called Wilbur at the hospital to tell on me. We have an internal phone system. She dialed two numbers, as she has seen all of us do. She happened to get the accounting office. In Spanish she said, "I want to talk to my father." The lady who works there asked, "Who is this?" Cristen answered in Spanish, "The Lewis daughter." By coincidence, Wilbur walked in at that moment. He took the phone and was stunned to hear his three-year-old break into a tirade against her mother for leaving her at home with Irma and Nilda. He told her he would be home later, so she was happy and hung up. The thing that bothered me is that sometimes I try for hours and can't find him down there.

Her speech is so funny with her little tongue having to master three languages. Her toy guitar has the comic character Archie on it so every guitar she sees is an Archie. We take her to hear harp/guitar musical groups and she calls them harps and Archies. Her swimsuit is her ba-zoot but she'd rather "swim in her tummy," the buff. She's singing now, and in honor of my star gazing she sings, "Twinkle, twinkle, little star, Mommie wonders what you are." Her favorite expression is "*¿Que hora es?* ('What time is it?')" It's funny to watch people's expressions with a three-year-old asking them that. Her best one to me was a couple of weeks ago while she and I were in the kitchen. She was chattering, then said, "Mommie, you look just like Jesus."

Tears stung my eyes at the impression parents make on their little ones and my heart swelled. I looked down at her, and she was looking at my feet. I had on my brown flat sandals. They do look just like the ones Jesus has on in our Sunday School pictures.

David is currently reading the Bible through. He told me last week, "Those daughters of Lot are awful! I bet I know what they are going to do. They're going to get their daddy drunk in that cave and run off and leave him." I decided to let the Spirit guide his understanding! I suppose that was right. He didn't say anything else about it. He told me that a miracle is something other people think you can't do but you do anyway. My favorite from David remains his reply to me years ago when Leanne was born.

I said, "Just think, David, we'll have to teach her all she knows."

"No, we'll have to teach her all she doesn't know."

Karen brought me to accounting recently. Once, in some of her endless questions of what and why, I told her the vertical depression above the upper lip was for mothers to rest their finger when they say, "Shhh." She said she believed that for years but finally realized daddies have it too, and they don't say, "Shhh."

Wilbur even gets cutesy from exposure to all the witty sayings. I had written an article for *Royal Service* and asked if he thought it would be too self-revealing to say a certain thing.

He said, "It's not a question of whether to reveal yourself or not. It's like buying a swimsuit. It's a question of whether or not you feel comfortable while you reveal yourself when you are all wet."

Me? I keep ten things going, but life is great. Think I must work better under pressure. Besides, that way the kids understand why I yell at them. It's hard on kids to be yelled at for no reason!

I LOVE YOU,
GLADYS

12
In Illness

Hepatitis Diary

Day Three

This is my third day of complete bedrest. I have acute hepatitis. Can't believe this has happened. The first two days I felt so bad I couldn't move. Today I am thinking of several weeks of this. I may go crazy. How to cope? Maybe if I write about it? Too much effort right now. So tired.

Day Six

Have to do something to feel in touch with life. Am isolated back here in my bedroom. Food is brought to the door. I take it on my dishes, try to eat, and rinse my things in the bathroom. Never thought eating would be difficult for me. Have set as a goal at least two pieces of meat each day and as much juice and water as I can tolerate without getting nauseated. Have decided to think of food as medicine since diet and bed rest are my only treatment.

How did this happen? Why? I don't have time for this. Stupid, stupid virus! Why did I have to swallow it! Why didn't my liver fight it off? Weak, stupid, idiot liver! Maybe I could prop some pillows and lean a book up to read. No strength to hold it. Don't think that will work. My neck muscles get tired of holding my head. In fact, my eye muscles get tired of holding my eyes. Am so angry, angry, angry, angry because my body will not do what I say.

Day Eight

Feel enough energy today to write a bit. Been thinking and sleuthing. Hepatitis is always around, but nobody in the Mission or in our church has it right now.

Question: Where was I six weeks ago, the time of the incubation period, from contact to symptoms? En route to Brazil with the family for vacation at Camboriu.

Question: How is contamination carried? By ingestion of the organism from a human carrier.

Question: Since we were all together for the two-three week period when I had to have received my contamination, why did I get it and they didn't? I ate something they did not.

Question: Did I go someplace the others did not? No.

Question: When did I eat something the others did not? At the restaurant where we ate when returning. They ate roast and I had shish kebab. Whoever prepared my shish kebab had hepatitis and gave it to me.

Question: Do I feel better? No!

Day Nine

Feel pretty good today until I stand. I'm tired of reading and sleeping. Need to exercise my brain.

Why am I so depressed about this? Hepatitis is not the end of the world. It's a calculated risk of living here or anywhere nowadays.

I'm mad because I'm sick. When I am sick, I'm out of my own control. I don't like that!

I'm mad also because I've been proved wrong. Always felt I could keep myself and mine well because I understand illness and have good health practices and precautions. In addition to my own knowledge, I did all that was suggested in orientation. In Costa Rica, in language school, I washed our fresh foods in potassium iodide before we ate them and cooked the rest thoroughly. We ate cabbage because its growth is inward and not contaminated and avoided lettuce because it grows outward and is unsafe. I boiled the water.

In fact, I have gone all over South America on two basic rules and have never been sick: 1. I don't eat lettuce if I don't *know* it's safe. 2. I don't drink unboiled water unless I *know* it's safe.

I keep thinking of Benson from language school. I've been

hard on him. He used to get under my skin making fun of my "food rituals," as he called them. He said he was not going to fool with all that. He believed God would take care of him.

I believe God will take care of me too, but I figure I can save him a little work for the heavier stuff if I knock off the bugs that will go away with routine procedures. Benson was very ill at one time. I felt awfully vindicated. However this puts a different slant on things.

It was a relief that Paraguay didn't have the problems of Costa Rica, and I don't have to go through those food processes. They even have a pure water system, thanks to US aid that built it. Only thing is, I hear the sewer line is going to be laid next to the water line. In a few years the water will be contaminated if they do that. Laying the water, then the sewer, sounds to me like putting on socks after the shoes are tied.

Wonder where Benson and Margaret are now. Is he pharisaical for thinking God would keep him healthy for the sake of his righteous ministry? That's what I thought of him. Maybe I was hypocritical for thinking I was better than Benson because of my sterling obedience and would end up receiving the greater blessing. It could be the opposite: he's the hypocrite and I am the Pharisee. Have to think about that. I do know I have sensed a pride for health that I considered my own product instead of gratitude for the gift it is.

Day Ten

Try this. If I know illness, diseases, and their causes and things to do to prevent them and do all that and stay well, I am OK. But if I don't stay well after doing all of it, where does that leave me?

It leaves me vulnerable, subject to danger I neither sense nor see. Am I my only defense? Where was God when I was served the hepatitis virus?

If I am vulnerable, if something can get me in spite of all I do, what am I to do then? Is this anger? No. Fear. I am afraid. If the hepatitis virus can get me, so can a lot of other things, all the way from dealing with me to dealing with other people.

Day Twelve

I don't like the ways enforced rest and isolation have made me look at myself. Plans and goals have really been my priority—more important than people. I have been short tempered and critical—not openly—but my thoughts could have raised a blister on the sun!

Question: Did God make me sick to have this encounter with my mind? No. I decided to order the shish kebab. He wasn't going to knock it off my plate with a thunderbolt once it was there. But he did set in action at the moment of ingestion forces that could bring me to the physical, emotional, and spiritual healing that I sense happening. Heavy thoughts for a weak, hepatitis body.

Need to think some more.

Day Fourteen

I have a conclusion. I have been reading the Gospel accounts of Christ's temptation. Have become absorbed by it. What does it all mean?

In my little corner, I can say I have been living on the mount of temptation and succumbing to all Christ resisted. That's not exactly the kind of mountaintop experience Baptists mean when they use the term.

Have been struggling with what the temptations were. As simply as I can pare it, this makes sense to me. The first was to take God's care into one's own hands; the second, to loll pridefully in unearned, unmerited power and prestige; and the third was to presume on God's care.

I have made lists of how I threw all these in a blender.

1. "I can take care of myself. I have already done it." I had adequate exposure on good health and health care. If you know how God does it, you can do it for yourself.

2. "I can always get up and go." An unhealthy body can't enjoy anything, especially a place of prominence, however it is acquired. Prior to gaining power, etc., is having the ability (e.g., health) to enjoy them. I have bragged about my strength. People have been sick about me and I chortle, "I have a stomach of iron" or

"Nothing makes me sick." Part of the rage I felt at the beginning of this was my inability to move myself. Four or five days before it was diagnosed, I could only drag from one chair to get enough strength to drag to another. It took the yellow in my eyes and fingernails to convince me that I was sick.

3. After the fact I said, "OK, God, straighten this out. I'll give you two days." I feel like I went ahead and jumped off the pinnacle and nobody caught me. I even feel like somebody came and made a trampoline of me after I landed.

What will I do differently? I'm not sure I have to do something. It is more what has happened inside me. Have a different attitude. I will certainly continue to take care of myself, but will never take health for granted or as evidence of my effort results. And I will be grateful to God for health knowledge, but treat it as a trust, not a possession. I plan to continue to enjoy this rock-ribbed constitution and strength of will that are mine, but will be aware I did not earn them. They are part of God's providence for some reason I don't understand, and do not plan to waste effort trying to understand.

I will appreciate more the existence of that which is beyond my awareness and control. But I won't live in fear. I claim in faith God's care for me in whatever comes.

I will rest in that.

Day Sixteen

My lab tests today were improved enough that I can begin to be up in a chair a few hours a day. If I show improvement, in two weeks I can begin to be out a half day with a half day of rest.

Lying in bed is not so bad now. I've done a backlog of intended reading. It is actually a luxury to read four and five hours at a stretch without a guilty conscience for letting something suffer that I should be working on. I have read Paul's letters from *A* to *Z*. Started Robertson's *Harmony of the Gospels* to redo the life of Christ. Want to take that slowly and think a lot.

Been reading Robert Ruark. *Uhuru* first, then *The Honey Badger*. Reminds me of Hemingway. Ernest the Wonderful . . . have a new paperback, *By-Line: Ernest Hemingway*. I am about halfway through it. Have gone shamelessly all over the world with him. His word colonies and communities nourish me with information, art, emotion. Bet I've read "Pamplona in July" ten times. Wonder if it's possible for a hepatitic missionary woman to have an "affair" with an old man through his books. Probably something in the Bible against it. Started yesterday on a project to read Aristotle. Will have to see how that goes. So far, he is not as entertaining as Ernest.

Think I will send word to Catalino to hang Che-Oro outside my window.

Day Seventeen

The two exciting hours in a chair turned out to be an hour and a half. Can't believe how weak I am.

Che-Oro was around for awhile this morning, but I had to send him back to the grape arbor. He kept screaming *"Mamita!"* at me to make our dog and deer quit chasing each other.

Now that I am allowed some time up, people are dropping by for a few minutes. It is wonderful to hear voices other than mine in my head.

They tell me of praying for me, which brings tears to my eyes and heart. I don't know if it gets God to do anything he had not already planned on, but it makes a difference in the way I feel. Like it is when you try really hard to learn a lesson, or a piece of music on the piano, something that is almost beyond you, and somebody without reason stops and says, "I know things are tough, but I'm with you."

Been thinking a lot about prayer. As far as prayer goes, I think God hears me as soon and as much as anyone, and he has certainly been hearing from me. As a matter of fact, I have more time to pray than the others right now. In fact, I wouldn't be surprised if God has a headache right now from my "much speaking!"

So why am I so touched by my colleague's prayers? It is not so much the end result of the act of their prayers as it is the act itself, that demonstration of their affection and love for me that is so good. In itself, it feels like little healing laser beams shining on my liver.

Bit off about fifteen minutes of Aristotle this afternoon and chewed on it for thirty. Am in Cuba with Hemingway hunting blue marlin. Started Taylor Caldwell's book on Cicero.

On an impulse, I got out my old love letters from Wilbur and read them today. Sigh. I want to tell him how sorry I am for all my faults, . . . am also amazed at how much worse he could have done. I may point that out as well.

Day Nineteen

Something strange has happened. *The Baptist Messenger* that came this week carried the news of the death of an OBU classmate of mine in Missouri. Cause of death? Hepatitis. It was like a message.

"Yes, you are recovering and doing well. But see what can happen with what you have? And it can happen anywhere."

I got into all kinds of questions like why him and not me, and wonder where he ate his "shish kebab."

I'll just say it out loud. With all the rest that has been in my mind the past two and a half weeks, I have thought about dying. And I am not ready to go, yet. There are too many things I want to do.

I always struggle with the phrases Christians pattern after Paul's talk about his eagerness to be with the Lord.

"I long to be with the Lord." Translation. "I am eager to die." Thing is, I'm with the Lord right now, and I don't want to die. The accepted nonverbal teaching in that is that spiritual people long to be with the Lord. The way to get there in that sense is to die.

I don't want to die. Never have. Never expect to.

We say heaven is better, and I believe it intellectually. But in the pit of my stomach, I really love what I have and I'm not lining up to trade it in.

I've heard sermons and biblical interpretations of the hereafter all my life. There are enough variations of views that I feel pretty much at home with heaven.

But once in awhile I have a nagging question. What if, when I get there, I discover we've missed some clue, and that which we have projected is not the way it is at all?

The big question I've never heard answered or even addressed is how all of us with so many emphatic, exact views on heaven are going to get along with each other when we get there. I don't doubt anybody's salvation, but some of the revelations about heaven get me curious.

I think missionaries will probably have a head start on it because of the practice in democratic communal living!

Death is not frightening to me. I just don't want to do it. When it does come, I think it will be like other experiences I have known of a progression from one reality to another, like marriage, parenthood, getting older. When it happens, I won't want to go back to a prior reality, life, any more than I now want to return to a previous life situation. Each present time is always the best for me. I think death will continue the pattern.

Day Twenty

I am reading Herman Wouk's, *City Boy*. Hilarious. Great medicine.

Also Paul. And Matthew, Mark, Luke, and John.

Big dose of Aristotle. The discussions of truth and knowledge turn my head inside out. Can all truths be demonstrated? Or is it truth? Is some knowledge independent of demonstration? I always take these things so personally. I am trying to demonstrate all the knowledge and truth I have by the way I am doing my life.

I stayed up the full two hours without problems today.

We got a big shipment of boat mail today with about six weeks worth of *The Sunday Oklahoman*. Great fun. Love the fashion sketches from Brown's. Wish my little Braniff wings could take me into the main store's perfume counter for a bottle of Faberge's Straw Hat.

Day Twenty-One

I am sitting at the window desk for my two hours today. It's a wonderful day! Gray, cloudy, and with a cool snap in the air! "Northers" here come from the south and the hot winds are from the north.

I'd appreciate the coolness if it blew straight down from up. We don't have air conditioning. Electricity prices rule that out. We do have a window unit for the bedroom, but never use it. If I can't have air conditioning all the time, I don't want it at all. It is worse to have a little bit, then none, than to do without completely.

I have a profound question for someone of capacity to answer. Why does hot air cooled feel better than cold air warmed?

Am just beginning Orwell's *1984*. Thing that bothers me is I know some folks who would think that was all right if the structures were Southern Baptist program parameters.

Day Twenty-Seven

Dona Blasida came to see me today. She is a saint.

We talked about communication with God, not prayer, but the way God talks to us.

Two times I have had supernatural experiences of direct God communication for very personal, private needs. Neither was of the nature that I could say "God told me. . . . " and deliver a message to a person.

But he does give me daily communication. It is most often and most practically through people. With alarming frequency he speaks to me and works for me through people who work against me. So far none has been the agent of Satan. Each has been a fellow believer.

For me, God's voice is a prism, slicing itself into many voices of harmony. I hear him most adequately and completely when I don't shut out any of the choirs that surround me, particularly the soloists with melodic dissonances of criticism.

The children seem to be surviving my absence from the front of the house. I have been so anxious about giving them this virus.

I am beginning to get mail from Oklahoma with expressions of interest and concern. Nice. Now that I have worked my way through the hard part, I can enjoy my invalidism!

Am staying up the full two hours and not wanting to return to bed when it's time. Feel stronger each day and have nothing but gratitude for it.

Have been intrigued by Aristotle's words on life, youth, and old age. Loved his saying there is a great discussion on whether the soul is located in the heart or the head! He'd feel right at home today. We still haven't figured it out.

Day Thirty

Two days ago I started getting up and out half a day. Wonderful! I'd forgotten how beautiful the world is. Lab tests continue to improve.

Get up at eight and do things around the house. And try to spend some time in the yard for strength and color. Catalino and Che-Oro are such wonderful companions.

A lot of desk work is piling up. Another day.

I go to bed at one in the afternoon and sleep three hours, then rest another hour. After a couple hours out with the family, I fall back in bed between eight and nine.

It's marvelous to be a part of the world of active life.

Day Thirty-Four

So little time for you, little diary. I am trying to catch up when I am up and sleep from fatigue when I am down.

Feel good, good, good.

Day Thirty-Nine

Will try to resume my classes at forty-two days if lab tests are all right. Worked on notes and lectures today. Reading time is vanishing. Am going to follow *1984* with Erich Fromm's *Escape from Freedom*. Have Jesus in Bethany and Paul in Corinth. I am glad Jesus is my Lord and Paul is my brother and not the other way around. Aristotle's ideas on anger, hate, and emotions remind me of Galatians. Bet Paul knew Aristotle's work as well as we know Paul's.

Want to start *Armageddon* and *The Arms of Krupp* before I am completely back in the swim, so I will have a study project not related to what I have to do.

Day Forty-Two

I'm pronounced well—with lots of admonitions about rest.

Strange Department! Wilbur told me they had a patient who died of hepatitis while I was sick.

Interesting I'd know about two deaths from a condition while I have it. I've heard people talk about deliverance from a situation that is fatal to someone else. The message unspoken, but hanging in the air, in the telling is that the preservation is due to the faith of the one preserved.

I don't know about the man in the hospital, but I do know I am not a person of greater faith than my friend in the States. Why me and not them? What does faith have to do with it, anyway?

I live by faith. Work by faith too. Like to carry my part of the load, even with the Lord.

God performs miracles, even for the undeserving, but not very often. Or it could be often, and the publicity is not so good in those cases. I give life my best shot always because I assume I won't be one of God's undeserved, effortless miracles. Maybe this time I am.

A couple of weeks ago, one of my visitors started me thinking about faith healing. The best act of faith for me when I am sick is to go to someone who has deeper healing knowledge than I and trust God to do the cure through that one who is in league with the way God has already set up healing to happen.

For me, it is more of a miracle for God to work through the minds of people to help them investigate, understand, and work with the healing process of medication, surgery, treatment, and control. More faith is required to trust that process, which I neither see nor understand, than to get someone to pray for me or lay hands on me.

God has put some smart folk in the healing business and the best ones have MD or RN after their names. My act of faith, trust to the unknown, is to be Christlike in the process, that is, obedient. I do exactly what I'm told.

I have long felt that medical healers of faith have to submit to more discipline and logical action than faith healers. If Wilbur did a work up on a patient and said, "Your tests indicate you need to have your gall bladder removed, but God told me to take out your thyroid, so I have you scheduled for a thyroidectomy at seven in the morning," the person would not think Wilbur was spiritual. The patient would assume he was a quack or worse. In the States, the closest malpractice lawyer would get a call within ten minutes.

My friend the other day wished there were miraculous healings like the ones in the New Testament. We don't have ones that match those, but we do have miraculous cures.

We don't heal twisted arms and legs, but with microsurgery and asepsis, severed limbs are reattached. We don't touch the blind and make them see, but we touch eyes with vacuum instruments and take away cataracts or transplant corneas and they see. We don't touch a woman with a twelve-year hemorrhage to stop the bleeding, but we have preventive health care and hysterectomy before such an extreme is reached.

There is one common factor between the New Testament miracles and ours—touch.

In the middle of the healing that Jesus did, devout people lived with pain, illness, and slow death. People of faith today live the same way while we go about our healing. We bring health to some in Paraguay, but there are many who don't receive what we offer. I don't know if all of those who do are deserving—or of faith.

We don't ask them those questions when they come. We don't do our work because of what is deserved. We do it because of who we are: servants with a service.

I think God's healing comes because of who he is, not because it is deserved. Neither the Bible nor God promises health. Instead, meaning and purpose are offered, a way to make some sense of life. For the great in the faith who suffer daily, meaning is in Christ, not physical well being.

Seems to me we always deal with the wrong issue in healing. We pump ourselves up with extolling what God can do instead of accepting what he does do and making the best we can of it.

God could have healed my friend and our patient here. I don't know why they died. But I'm certain of my life—and how uncertain it is. I accept it with joy for today and plan to give and get the best I can.
Day Fifty

I really am well. Back on schedule. The doxology rings in my head each time I walk outside. It would surely be nice to have a day in bed sometime!

13
In Missionary Households

"Smile!" Lights flash. "Good picture!" Wilbur snaps on the shutter cover. Our toddler stands from the package she was examining under the Christmas tree and lifts her arms to the two bright-eyed Paraguayan girls.

"She wants to go to the party with us, *Senora*," Nilda says. The unspoken question is, "May we take her?"

"She just wants you to carry her around. You go on to the church. She'd have your dresses and your pretty hairdos mussed before you got out the gate. Scat! Have fun."

They click across the tile floor, unaccustomed to high-heeled shoes, and fade into the soft darkness through the door that opens onto the hot December night.

I pick up Cristen. "Come here, Tootie. Let's rock a little."

Wilbur asks, "Why is she awake and everyone else is in bed?"

"She slept all afternoon. The heat, I guess."

He looks toward the open door. "Funny. They seem more like our daughters now than maids."

"They act more like daughters than maids. I feel the three of us have a commitment. They help me. I help them."

"Has Nilda paid for her sewing machine yet?"

"Two more months."

"I never thought it would work when you wanted to take her too. In helping her buy the machine, I felt sure we were making a mistake."

"She came to the city to go to the seamstress school, but when she finished she couldn't work at her profession until she had a machine."

"It was a risk—two sisters."

"The basic decision was to keep Irma. With her going to school, it was like having five children: four little kids and a sixteen-year-old."

His eyes crinkle. "So you solved it by getting an eighteen-year-old."

"They are wonderful to the children. I'm teaching them to cook."

"Going to include a course on your reasoning?" Wilbur teases. "Like?"

"Giving them a raise so their tithe will be increased and their church's stewardship campaign will be helped. . . . "

"I . . . "

"And so that they will have a little more for themselves after Irma's school fees and Nilda's machine payments are taken out of their salaries," he continues verbalizing what I had thought when I gave the raises.

"Good business practice," I interject.

"Oh?" he questions.

"If they are happy, I am happy."

"With those two conditions, so am I."

"Between the three of us we cover everything. The best part is they do it my way," I explain.

"We've had some real encounters."

"More like revolving doors. Remember the German girl who stayed a week, cried the whole time, and wouldn't tell me what was wrong?"

"My favorite was Liduvina. I still can't believe you would not let her eat desserts."

"She had no self-control! She would eat it all of whatever dessert had been prepared while we had our meal. I put up with it until that night the Kintners were here," I explain.

"I'll never forget the look on your face when you brought that tray in with two pieces of pie and said, 'You're not going to believe this,'" Wilbur laughs.

I join him. We laugh so hard the baby leans back to look me in the face, then laughs with us.

"I probably wouldn't have been so mad, but I made that pie with cherries and Crisco I'd brought from the States."

"She was the champion."

"She ate three pieces of pie while I was in here getting out the china!"

Wilbur catches his breath and says, "I'm glad you finally got past feeling you shouldn't have help."

"My puritan work ethic. My mother didn't have help. Her mother didn't have help."

"Households here involve more work."

"I had to decide, finally, if God called me to be a missionary or to mop these clay tile floors every day with that square mop cloth thrown over the wooden mop stick so I could tell everybody who cared, which was no one, that I do all my own work," I say.

"A household is more than the immediate family here."

"It's everybody who lives under the same roof."

"And some who don't," Wilbur says, then waits for me to think of who he has in mind.

"Catalino?"

"He's grown up with us."

"Been sort of a shared son between the Watsons, Skinners, and Lewises."

"He was fourteen when we first came."

"He was one of the first Paraguayans I met. He came to see me at the Skinner's house the day after we arrived to ask if he could work for us. You were at the hospital with all that freight. The lawn was the last thing on my mind."

"He's been a constant part of our household since then, except the year he was drafted."

"I shall never adjust to sixteen year olds being drafted."

"The government considers them to be in their seventeenth year when they have their sixteenth birthday, so they have to register then."

"If Liduvina was your favorite, mine was that fellow you hired to cut the grass who set the storeroom on fire building a blaze to make his *maté*!"

"Nobody's perfect," Wilbur shrugs.

"Some don't come close!" I exclaim.

"I was happy Catalino took the sweltering Chaco service which shortened his military year to seven months," Wilbur continues. "I thought for a while I was going to have to cancel surgery and push the lawn mower."

"Trade your scalpel for a *machete*?"

"When he went to register, he was taken right then. Didn't have time to tell us."

"But we are so wise! We figured it out."

"He reappeared seven months later to the date."

"I saw him at the gate before he clapped and flew out there and grabbed him. I felt like my son had come home. Mariana was here when I brought him in to show him the baby. She gasped when he said, '*Senora!* I didn't even know we were pregnant! *Una nenita!*'"

"He got pretty tired of the *nenita* stripping off her clothes and running around in the buff in his flowers."

"At first he'd call me to come get her. Then he'd just bring her in one arm, her clothes in another, and say, '*Senora*, again,'" I chuckle.

Cristen relaxes against me. "This little pet is asleep."

"Where is that little pet's little pet?"

"Princess? Bedded down with Duchess, I suppose."

"Did you get by without giving the deer the bottle today?"

"No. I don't know how we'll wean her. She throws a temper fit if Cristen doesn't give her the bottle, and Cristen has a tantrum if I don't let her have the bottle to give to Duchess. That deer comes to the back door on schedule and cries until she gets her bottle."

"Milk won't hurt her."

"It's just unnatural for a half-grown deer to order a nursing bottle of milk at the back door."

"Maybe you could teach her to clap at the front gate?"

"Che-Oro would take care of that."

"Wanda does keep us supplied!"

"When she isn't thinking up new classes for me to teach at the nursing school, she's collecting animals for me."

"You'll never get Anatomy from me! That's my claim to fame. Dr. Wilbur Lewis, professor of Anatomy."

"Sweetheart, consider your title safe."

"The nurse in the Chaco who sent Duchess to Wanda in the New Tribes plane was in my first anatomy class."

"Bet that's how she recognized it as a deer."

"Couldn't be, I stuck to people."

"She sent word to Wanda with the fawn that the mother had been killed. I'm sure the pilot was tickled to put her in the plane and bring her here!"

"By the time Wanda got her here, the fawn was nearly starved."

"It was so frustrating trying to find some way to get food into her. I just happened to remember those two old baby bottles."

"Where'd Wanda get Che-Oro?"

"Somebody gave him to her. He's a pretty old bird—thirtyish she says."

"He's a one-woman fellow—like me!" says Wilbur, referring to the fact that Che-Oro has become *my* pet.

"We understand each other."

"He nearly broke your finger when he bit you."

"I scared him when I stuck my hand in his cage to get his bowl. We were still new to him."

"You were crying from the pain."

"He came out on my shoulder, stroked my cheek, and said he was sorry."

"You lost the fingernail."

"I got over it."

"What's a fingernail when there is love!"

I rock and look at the braided rug. Wilbur lies back on the sofa, hands behind his head, staring at the ceiling.

"Remember when Bill Hickman had me come to cut the tails off his terriers?"

"Can I ever forget Amigo?"

"At least he didn't give me Old Twist."

"Amigo was probably the only dog in canine history who could stand flat-footed and jump twelve feet. You kept putting barricades on the back fence to keep Amigo in. The Skinners and I kept taking it down. I wanted him to run away. They didn't want a kid to get killed if the barricade fell."

"Don't be harsh on Amigo. He got you a gentleman friend."

"If I'd been smart, I would have let him follow the milkman that day."

"At this very moment, there probably sits in this city a lonely milkman, composing a *guarania* about a *linda gringa* who called him softly, 'Amigo, Amigo,' but changed her mind when he rushed to her side and broke his heart with a story about calling her puppy!"

I grab the pillow beside me and throw it at him. "As far as I am concerned, Princess is a welcome replacement."

"Still protective of her food?"

"Fiercely. Stands astraddle her food bowl, even empty, with her lip up just a bit. We all go about our business with her guarding her pan."

"Does she growl or bark?"

"Stands silently on duty with teeth visible."

"Maybe being a blond cocker with parents from Japan makes you show your teeth, like being a terrior named Amigo makes you follow milkmen and jump over walls."

"How would you account for a parrot who sings with the harp teacher and a deer who asks for a baby bottle?"

"No explanation, just a bond," Wilbur says.

"Which is?"

"That which ties Irma, Nilda, and Catalino to this household."

"And that is?"

"We love them. They love us," he concludes.

"And I love you."

"I feel like Joshua. 'As for me and my house, we will serve the Lord.'"

I stand with the limp little one sleeping against me. "As for me and my house, we are going to bed!"

14
In Interpersonal Relationships

We step carefully on the bars of the cattle guard that line the gate from the street into the hospital property. The presence of the guard makes it difficult for people to get in. The cows jump across.

Turning down the road between the church and the school building, we walk toward our house. My adrenaline is up and raging. So is my mouth.

"I did *not* think we should have voted to do that!" We crunch along. The soft darkness of the Paraguayan night parts to let us by.

"Mission meetings give me a pain!" I add and look up at my partner. He walks with one hand in his pocket, the other around my shoulder, and does not answer. We turn into our house. "Did you think we should have voted to do that?"

"Nope."

"OK, Gary Cooper! How can you be so calm about it?"

"I figure they can talk to God the same as I can."

Stung, I keep my thoughts to myself. He squeezes my shoulder, and we enter the living room. The lamp by the gold chair is on low and spills lemon-colored light in a circle on the floor. The mail is lying on the coffee table. He picks up the letters and the current *Time*.

"These are all to you. GA's?"

"Two are. One is from Phyllis. Chatty stuff."

He drops them where they were. "I'll read *Time* later. Got a big case at seven in the morning."

"I'm not sleepy. I think I'll read a while."

"Sure." He starts to the hall, then turns back. "It'll be OK."

"I know."

The gold chair has a red truck on the edge of its seat cushion. I pick up the truck, sink into the chair, and stare through the room toward the backyard. From the hall comes the soft sleeping sounds that children make and the noise of toothbrushing from beyond. With an effort, I place the truck on the table and pick up *Time*. I flip through it and pitch it beside the truck. Moscow and Washington have been at it all my life and will continue after I'm gone. I don't care to read about their latest chapter tonight. Something heavier than international conflict occupies me.

The moon is up. I stand and head toward the back door. The white outline of a wooden platform, free-standing swing waits in the yard. The ancient Jews had the Temple, the holy place, and the holy of holies, where they reconciled themselves with God. I have my swing. I had it built for that purpose.

The Hebrews were reconciled through sacrifice and ceremony on feast days and holy days. I make my peace with God through thinking and rocking, wrapped in the Paraguayan night when my world and responsibilities are in bed.

Slouching across the seat for two, I pull my feet under me and cradle my head with my arms. My weight in the swing starts a gentle rocking, and I watch the full moon steadily increase its distance from the top of the wall in its climb up the eastern sky.

My holy of holies that never had a veil begins to work its ministry, and relaxation eases through me.

I try to focus on the cause of my restlessness. It started during Mission meeting tonight. All the missionaries in Paraguay are together for our annual meeting: budget study, personnel requests, review of reports, inspiration time, and seeing all the children.

I rock.

"I want to thank you for these people you let me work with," I say to God. He pushes the moon up another two inches while I watch. It develops a watery edge and I wipe my eyes to get it back in line.

"The truth is, if you would let me search through the world to pick a group to share this kind of life with, I'd pick each one of them," I blurt to God.

He waits.

I swing.

"You know I love them. They are other parts of myself."

Silence.

I kick my feet out and straighten up, throwing the swing into violent movement.

"Then why am I so mad at them?"

My perch slows to gentler rocking, and I think through the events of the meeting and my report before the vote. Yahweh of the Day of Atonement blows aside the smoke from my altar and meets me.

"They chose not to do it my way!"

Reconciliation snaps into place with understanding.

Missionaries are leaders, performers, achievers. They have to be to get appointed. With twenty-two or fifty or one hundred and fifty working together for one purpose, with dozens of ways to get to the goal, with each having a personal calling to achieve the purpose, and each with a direct pipeline to God's will in every matter, majority rule is the only way to work together. One person/one vote is the great equalizer for all things great and small, base or profound, pragmatic or theological.

"The issue is never the issue," I say to God. "The issue is my reaction to the issue."

The moon glides past a lonely cloud that evaporates with the passing. I see the Southern Cross, study briefly the rough diamond-shaped constellation, and reflect on my disappointment in it. I didn't expect a neon outlined cross flashing, "Jesus Saves," but there ought to be something more definite than what is there with such a good name.

"On Top of Old Smoky" begins to hum in my head.

I learned the first year here that the only thing I can change about people and situations is my attitude toward them. Three things help me do that: a trip out to the swing, a little time, and a hearty belly laugh.

I tell God news that isn't new. "As soon as I can laugh about this, I'll be all right."

On an impulse I go to the back door, slip out of my shoes, pad through the house, carefully open my closet, feel for my ukulele, slip back past sleeping bodies to the kitchen. I step into my shoes and glide back to my sanctuary.

Cherubim and seraphim waiting for psaltery hymns hear a ukulele chord.

> On top of old Smoky
> All covered with snow
> Is a mental hospital
> With lights all aglow.
> It has all kinds of patients
> From all walks of life
> But *the* biggest problem
> Is a missionary's wife.

Well into my first year here, I finally realized it is all right to laugh at the mission field. I did it first by laughing at myself with this autobiographical song. After thirty-seven verses at one of our Mission meetings, we were rolling on the floor and I was on my way to adjustment.

I strum through some of my favorite verses.

> She went to the doctor
> For him to help her
> But all that he'd offer,
> Was a tranquilizer.

> She talked with her pastor
> At the top of her lungs
> But she felt his counsel
> Was spoken in tongues.

Her husband consulted
With friends far and wide
Results were tremendous
Gossip still hasn't died.

The release I give myself through humor, I share with my colleagues. It is a safety valve for all of us. I catalog in song some of what is mine to do.

"I work hard, God. I really like my job. I do a lot, but I think what I do best is make people laugh."

The moon glows brighter.

The faces of my colleagues take turns as substitutes in the face of the moon for the man usually there. My missionary brothers and sisters are my neighbors, my work partners, my cultural colony in the midst of an adopted country, my fellow church members. If I play, I play with them. When I fight, I fight with them.

"You know what, Lord? They are just like what you said about the poor. They are *always* with me! They are my family in the faith and surrogate family in the flesh."

I watch their faces shifting in the moon spotlight. I feel like God is lifting the cloud that tries to veil my view of myself and my colleagues.

"Matter of fact, they're like what you said about yourself. When I rise up in the morning, they are there; when I lie down in the evening, they are there."

An insomniac breeze rustles a few leaves in the avocado tree. I nudged that tree into existence by putting an avocado seed in a glass of water until the tree burst from its shell as an eager plant; then I placed it in the warm wet earth one Easter to celebrate the new birth.

"I guess that's the best part. They *are* like you. And they are here. And I *love them so much*."

A personal, little constellation I named the Christmas Tree edges up over the wall.

"And they love me!"

I strum a few chords of "America the Beautiful" and sing softly a chorus.

> Asuncion, Asuncion,
> We dedicate our pills!
> They're no account,
> We don't give discount,
> We doubt they'll cure your ills.

The Christmas Tree wheels around the sky as close to the moon as it ever comes. A star tree cannot come close to the moon. Its service is as a symbol of wood that is made into the swing where heart altars receive self-preferment sacrifices and give back reconciliation in laughter.

My uke-psalter lazes through several of my own psalm-hymns.

"Anyway, Lord, sometimes when I lose, I win." I begin to strum "Greensleeves" and remember our return from furlough. Our house was fenced from the main street. The back wall was opened, which meant extra dust, mud, and travel everytime I came and went. I sing a bit of it.

> Alas, dear friends, you did do me dirt,
> Stuck a knife in my back, you did make me hurt,
> When a year ago you did come to meet,
> And voted to fence my house from the street.
> Red, red is all I see
> When the clouds hang low
> And the rain falls free.
> Red, red is all I see,
> When I think what you did here to me.

The fence was gone in a week.

I lean forward, place the uke on the seat opposite, and stretch lazily against the swinging seat. The Christmas Tree guards its turf from the other stars, keeping its space from them to maintain visibility. I shift my view a bit to see the Southern Cross and act more respectfully. "The wooden one down here wasn't pretty, either. But what happened on it defines beauty for eternity."

The details of the evening's decision crowd in on my Star Cross talk.

"It's not a bad plan, Lord. Fact is, it's a good plan. Anyway, now that it's voted, it's my plan too."

I bend forward and lift the ukulele from its covenant ark.

"I need to bring some closure to it." I begin to finger the fret and "There Is a Tavern in the Town" materializes. I experiment.

> A Mission meeting in this town,
> Where holy people sat them down. . . .

I hug the uke, slap my knee, and laugh out loud.

"They'll love it!" I whisper-yell to the moon. The moon glows, and my awareness of God's presence in my life and work grows. I blink and look again at the face of the man in the moon. The uke wood is smooth and worn where my arm holds it. I pat the swing and give it a little shove with my foot.

"I could have sworn he winked."

15
In Mission Field Organization

"Mother."

I look up from my desk. My very own Cub Scout stands framed in the doorway.

"I'm going to meet with Aunt Betty. She wants to know if you can help me set up my Cub Alone display tonight?"

"Sure."

He looks at the desk. "Are you doing your Mission or Convention stuff this afternoon?"

"Mission."

"May I stay and play with Charlie a while?"

"Be fine." He turns from me. "Have fun, Bodge," I call to his footfalls.

Wilbur sticks his head in the door. "It's back to work."

"For me too."

He steps into the room. "Do you think we ought to quit calling him that? I'm afraid he'll get a nickname."

"He has it!"

"I didn't like my nickname." He walks to the door.

"I don't blame you!"

"To the salt mines!"

"Viva Geritol!"

Bodge! I shake my head. Cristen thinks I am calling David when I say, "Time to eat, everybody," because David is the one immediately in place. She pronounces *everybody* as *'bod-gee*. We have shortened it and him to *Bodge*.

I turn in my chair to the bookshelves. They are organized the way my life is: Mission, church, Convention, hospital and nursing school.

The church section has the treasurer's materials, Sunday School supplies and pictures. Convention has the education board's papers and hospital board reports. Nursing school and hospital parts hold nursing texts and notes and lectures and files on *Hoplita,* the in-service newsletter I edit for the employees.

With my heels, I push the roller chair to the Mission shelf. It is divided by tabs taped to the wood: assistant secretary, handbook, policy book, personnel committee. A larger section is marked chairman. Wilbur is serving his second year in that office.

It is always hard for me to explain to people at home what the Mission is. Convention is understandable. Church certainly is. Hospital board is not a mystery. Nursing school is plain enough. But the Mission has no stateside corollary.

It is to the Foreign Mission Board what an embassy is to the US Government, the representative agent of the Board in another country. As an embassy is the visible presence of the American people in a country through reflecting the aims and policies of the US Government, so the Mission reflects Southern Baptists in a country and projects and interprets hopes and visions of the Foreign Mission Board.

Embassies reflexly explain local governments to Washington and Missions initiate cooperative endeavors from the field that connects with overall policy in Richmond.

Everything a missionary does is geared toward the central purpose of bringing the gospel to the people of his field. He or she does it dozens of ways through parallel organizations and structures with interacting and overarching connections.

Missionaries work in churches and the Convention. They also have organizational responsibilities within the Mission.

I have a combination of several jobs: assistant secretary, handbook officer, reporter, and a committee assignment.

I run my finger along the files to pull out the minutes notebook and hesitate at a bulky file labeled mock minutes, songs, and korn.

My functional work as assistant secretary is a prescribed routine of
recordkeeping that relates to our handbook. My ministerial work is
the mock minutes.

The Mission records before me represent years of planning,
projecting, and record keeping.

Missionaries are doers. They are better at doing than they are at
keeping records of what was done.

Long meetings are dull and very short on inspiration. When
missionaries talk about their work in planning sessions, the language is conceptual, matter of fact, rarely spiritualized. To lift the
load, focus attention, and let in a little light, the mock minutes come
among us, "divinely inspired" probably.

I lift one folder and read one set.

April Mission Meeting

JIM: Well, let's see now. . . . It's about time to get started. Let's kick
this thing off with a prayer. Who hasn't done it yet this year?
Who's that hiding under the table? Wanda, will you lead us in
prayer?
(Wanda prays.)
Now, then, where were we? Or do we have a quorum? Frances
Skinner is not here yet. Who is our assistant secretary? Betty
Harper, you take notes.

BEVERLY: Mr. President. . . .

JIM: Beverly . . .

BEVERLY: Could we postpone the reading of the minutes until the
secretary arrives?

JIM: I'm sorry. We can't discuss that. We don't have a motion on the
floor.

BEVERLY: Couldn't we just agree to do so by common consent?

JIM: I don't know. It's all right with me. What does the group want
to do?

BILL: Mr. President . . .

JIM: Just a minute now. Let's make a list of those who want to talk.

Bill Hickman. Leland Harper. Wanda Ponder. Anybody else? OK. Bill.

BILL: I just want to say that I remember talking with Dr. Means twelve, no, eleven years ago on this matter, and he said it's perfectly all right for a Mission to do what it thinks best.

JIM: Here are the Lewises. Gladys, will you take our minutes? Now, where are we? It's Leland's turn. Betty, you want on the list too? OK.

LELAND: I would like to see us do this and I have thought that we will need to do it. I don't really care when we do it, but I'd like to invite the nationals to study this with us.

JIM: Thank you, Leland. I think it is good that we are expressing ourselves. It is very good to talk these things over. Bill Hickman, you want on the list again? And Gladys. Anybody else? Now it is Wanda's turn.

WANDA: What are we talking about?

JIM: Folks, now let's pay attention. I remember once in Argentina I wasn't listening to the discussion, and I voted with the group on something. It was a unanimous vote for me to start work in Tierra del Fuego.

LELAND: Jim, we don't want to get you heated.

JIM: You're right. I just wanted to throw a little light on things.

WANDA: What are we talking about?

JIM: Wanda, we are discussing whether we can agree to postpone the reading of the minutes by common consent since we can't discuss the actual postponement because we don't have a motion.

WANDA: Oh.

JIM: Let's see. Bill, Gladys, May McDowell, Jane Hickman.

BETTY: I was on that list a long time ago.

JIM: I'm sorry. Go ahead, Betty.

BETTY: That's all right. I forgot what I was going to say.

BILL: I know we are pressed for time, but I think these things are important and need to be thought through. I would personally like to see us *not* discuss this because I don't think we ought to hurry into any decisions. I remember. . . .

JIM: All right, thank you. May.

MAY: I think minutes are nice.

JIM: That's a point well taken. Jane.

JANE: What kind of minutes are they?

JIM: Mission minutes. Wait now, we overlooked Gladys.

GLADYS: In the handbook under "Mission, Organization of," p. 80, no. (6) under d. "New policies," we have a letter from Dr. Means requesting that minutes be approved after each meeting to get to the Board sooner. Now if that is Board policy, I think we ought to read them.

JIM: Mack.

MACK: Now, I'm going way out on a limb. I'm going in in deep water, and I may drown. I don't have my committee to back me up, but I'm going to make a motion. I'm going to throw it out and see if anyone picks it up. Here it is: In view of the fact that the mission was established in 1951, one hundred and six years after the Southern Baptist Convention, and since the Southern Baptist Convention established by precedent the reading of minutes, I move that we set the general policy of reading minutes of the Mission in Mission meeting.

JIM: All right! Is there a second?

WILBUR: I'll second it if we insert "writing and" before reading and add at the bottom, "whether the secretary is or is not present and that the Mission establish a committee on Mission minutes and that the committee give its report while Dr. Smith is here.

JIM: All right. Gladys. Then Bill.

GLADYS: But we already have a policy about minutes. I'm sorry, but my conscience bothers me.

BILL: I would just like to say that I think we ought to be very careful about doing. . . .

JIM: Thank you, Bill. Beverly?

BEVERLY: If we approve this, does it mean the Journeymen get copies of the minutes?

JIM: Yes, I would think so.

WILBUR: Question!

JIM: Those in favor—three. Against—two. Abstaining—ten! Motion fails to pass for lack of a two-thirds majority of those voting. We won't read the minutes.

MARIE: I'd just like to ask if this means we won't ever at all read them.

GLADYS: The handbook says we have to!

(Enter Bill and Fran Skinner.)

JIM: Could we by common consent agree to have the minutes read? Let's have an informal vote. Fourteen, for, one, against. OK. Read the minutes.

FRAN: The PMB of the FMB of the SBC met at 2 PM with all present except Leland Harper, who was on chauffeur detail and Bill Skinner who had gone to check the hospital. The minutes of the previous session were read after a discussion as to whether or not they should be read before or after the Bible reading and prayer.

The chairman called for an election of a temporary chairman because he will be out of the country during the annual mission meeting on business for the book deposit and the present vice-chairman feels that in order to preside at annual mission meeting a vice-chairman should have special mission approval.

Leland Harper returned to the meeting at this time and was elected, but Betty Harper proposed the reasons why he could not serve. He withdrew.

Mack Jones was elected, but he asked for the floor stating that because of recent committee studies he cannot serve, but that while he is talking, if he thinks of anything to say he will mention it. Since his election would mean missing his furlough, he felt it would be better for the Mission not to sink a ship to drown a rat.

May McDowell proposed the name of Gilbert Nichols, but Betty Harper pointed out to her that the Nichols are on furlough. May withdrew her nomination.

Bill Skinner returned to the meeting at this time.

Wilbur Lewis announced that he could have served, but that his duties as Asuncion Christian Academy representative prevent his doing so now.

Betty Harper left the meeting.

On the second ballot, Bill Hickman was elected temporary chairman. He stated that he did not feel that he could serve because his wife is a member of the Mission.

Betty Harper returned to the meeting.

May McDowell left the meeting.

On the third ballot, Wanda Ponder, May McDowell, and Beverly Lutz tied.

May hurriedly returned to the meeting. She and Beverly refused because of furlough plans.

Leland did not feel that the Mission should ask a woman to be chairman.

Mack Jones demanded equal time to speak against Wanda.

On the fourth ballot, there was a tie between eight blank ballots and eight marked with a question mark. The chairman referred the matter to a special committee on motions for a further study to be returned to a special meeting with recommendations. After considerable discussion as to who will serve on the committee, the naming of the committee members was postponed to a later date.

The chairman called on Dr. Hoke Smith for report on the recent field representative meeting.

Dr. Smith stated that he had five or six pages on TV work, but that he would not go into it except to say that we do have TV work. He mentioned that a church development survey committee for Latin America has been appointed and that they have already ascertained that in all countries where we have work, there are now churches.

He stated that the most important thing is the reorganization of the administrative department of the FMB. Dr. Means feels that this is the most important and significant development in Latin America since Roberta Fleitas won the track meet in Buenos Aires.

In connection with his discussion on the Board's decision to computerize procedure, he passed out keypunch cards to every member of the mission. He pointed out the following:

The large number in the center deals with salary, business, and freight.

The small red numbers on the right deal with the Margaret Fund.

The small blue numbers on the right deal with furlough.

The small green numbers on the right deal with deputation.

He said the missionary should not feel that the board is depersonalizing and that he should feel free to write at anytime. The small black numbers on the left corner are the correspondence code he should use when writing. However, should there be some item to discuss not covered in the items on the card, the missionary should *not write*. He added that the missionary should not lose his card because all his data is on microfilm, and the board cannot find the missionary without the computer card.

Mack Jones stated that he was not trying to shift us into second gear, but that he did feel hemmed up by all this and that we mustn't go into this for a horse swap. Since the board has approved the computer system, Mack stated that he would like to request information on what would be board policy if the missionary lost his card.

Dr. Smith said that while the Mission certainly could express their reactions to what the board had decided, they, the Mission, should express their feelings in writing to the board and that he would try to interpret these to the board, but that at the same time he was also charged with interpreting the board's policy to the Mission, and that the board had decided in the event that a missionary loses his computer card, he will have to resign and start all over.

Mack Jones stated that he had swung for a bunt and knocked a home run.

At this moment, Wilbur Lewis brought up a point of order. Bible reading and prayer had been postponed until after the reading of the minutes.

Dr. Smith suspended his report.

The chairman read the Bible, somewhere in the New Testament. Wilbur Lewis led in prayer.

The floor was returned to Dr. Smith. He stated that was all of his report.

The chairman asked for the camp administrator's report and the handbook report. There were thirty-three single-spaced pages as the handbook entries were for the past three years and the camp administrator's report covered five studies he had been asked to make. The motion was made by Bill Hickman, seconded by (who seconded that? Leland did. . . . No, I didn't. . . . Wilbur did . . . No, Beverly did . . . I didn't, but you can use my name . . . Don McDowell, "I did.") Don McDowell, to refer the reports to a committee to study.

There was an amendment to the motion, Wilbur Lewis, Marie Jones, to bring the study to the July meeting.

A substitute motion was made, Leland Harper, Mack Jones, to delete the reports altogether.

The vote by secret ballot was fourteen in favor, two opposed. Bill Skinner and Gladys Lewis, camp administrator and handbook officer, left the meeting in protest.

Mack Jones stated he had written Dr. Means about deleting reports and expected to have a reply by the next meeting.

The meeting adjourned at 6:45 PM.

JIM: You have heard the minutes. They stand approved as read. We will go to the property committee report.

MACK: The only thing left is the matter of the curtain to keep the light out of the darkroom at the *senoritas*' apartment.

FRAN: Is that a recommendation?

MACK: Yes.

JIM: Is there a motion?

DON: I so move.

FRAN: Write it out. *(Don writes it.)*

JIM: Will the secretary read the motion?

FRAN: "I so move."

MACK: It's just like it's printed.

FRAN: I don't have that. It's already been changed three times.

MACK: I'll make a substitute motion. I move that in light of the fact that there is light in the darkroom at the *senoritas'* apartment that we put a curtain at the window and if this is approved that we request a reallocation to pay for the curtain.

BETTY: I'll second it if we can also include the guest apartment.

FRANCES: Would this be all the windows in the guest apartment?

JIM: Maybe the committee could make a note of this to include in their next study.

BILL: I'd like to speak.

JIM: Is it related to this?

BILL: Let me say what I'm going to say, then you'll know what I want to say. I think we should.

JIM: All in favor? Unanimous! Now, personnel-health-transportation committee report.

WILBUR: No. 1 on page 3 first, then 3 on page 5—then go back to page 1 for 4. . . .

WANDA: I'm against it! Single people get less.

MACK: Is this to the States only or from? Or should it be going and returning? How about "to, from, and while en route?"

JIM: Why don't we make a study?

MAY: I move that Beverly and Wanda get married so they can have equal baggage allowance.

WANDA and BEVERLY: Second!

WILBUR: I move that we recommend to the board that baggage rates remain the same but that missionaries get to see the first-class movies.

GLADYS: I'd like to make a substitute motion that missionaries get double baggage allowance *and* travel first class.

BEVERLY: Mr. Chairman! I accuse the Lewises of pork barrel politics and collusion. He makes a motion no one can stand. She makes an opposite one and everyone is so relieved to have a choice that the Lewises get what they want anyway!

MACK: I move that the board pay all baggage costs anytime, anywhere!

ALL: Second! *(Unanimous vote follows.)*

FRAN: Is that a comma or a semicolon between anytime and anywhere?

JIM: Comma. Now, Wilbur has eleven legal size pages on emotional, that is, constitutional amendments.

FRAN: I'd like to make a motion. I move that we strike out the constitution.

JIM: All in favor? Unanimous! We'll adjourn without a prayer.

With laughs and giggles I flip through several other sheets and see one outlining plans for a parade of the missionaries to show support for the Crusade of the Americas. After several months of minute and detailed plans for the big intercontinental crusade, we let in some air and breathing space with this bit of nonsense.

In order to show our love and support of the Crusade of the Americas, we, the Baptist Mission in Paraguay, present the following plan for our part in the parade in downtown Asuncion that will kick off the campaign year.

First, for two weeks before the parade we will meet every day at the Plaza Uruguaya to practice arriving on time. This will also give the hospital and the theological institute ample warning that we are up to something special and should not be bothered at that hour except for extreme emergency.

The second step calls for all missionaries to march in a block or group since this is the way we almost always vote. This will also help to avoid showing favoritism to the churches where we are members and spare embarrassment to other churches which do not have missionaries in their fellowships. It would also be a positive support for our missionary-national relationships.

In a further effort, we will prepare a sign four by twenty meters that has the crusade logo and Scripture. The two men who will carry the banner will be selected by preferential secret ballot.

Gladys Lewis has been commissioned to paint the sign. Funds for four hundred magic markers, paint, and national fabric have been reallocated from the library fund.

Wilbur Lewis, as mission chairman, has been asked to carry an open Bible at the head of the group. It is a special edition in *Guarani* just for the crusade year that was purchased with petty cash from the theological institute board.

The group will be preceded immediately by the mobile clinic with loudspeakers playing that grand old hymn, "The Fight Is On." Just behind the sign the group will march in the following order with the equipment symbolic of their work:

Fran Skinner with the Mission records on a hospital kitchen tray cart; Bill Skinner with a specially-designed coat made from old EKG recordings and a stack of *For Rent* signs for the Home Mission Board's pastors' homes tied together with umbilical tape; Jim Watson with a mobile pastoral counseling clinic and bundles of audiovisual materials tied together with the red tape he loves to cut; Frances Watson with three copies of the *Dewey Decimal System* and four albums of her grandsons' pictures; Jane Hickman with all the WMU manuals from 1953 to the present in her market baskets; Bill Hickman with his institute records camouflaged in a bale of hay; Leland Harper with his portable treasurer's office and 379,000 copies of John 3:16 printed on his own personalized prescription pads; Betty Harper in her complete nurse uniform except for a Sherlock Holmes hat and magnifying glass; and Wanda Ponder who will also march in her nurse uniform and carry her dilapidated (from disuse) fishing pole, which will have a leash so Pompideaux can also march.

Immediately behind the group will be a float constructed on the flatbed of the hospital ambulance, the flatbed being the result of a sudden stop in front of a cargo truck. The float will be decorated with a motif created by stuffing of old secret ballots in chicken wire. It will carry Miss (or Mrs.) Missionary, alias Miss (or Mrs.) Crusade of the Americas. Selection requirements are being studied by a special committee. In the event that a consensus is not reached, the float will parade without anyone on it as a symbol of our spiritual excellence and rejection of such worldly pursuits.

Replacing the papers and the folder, I lift the minutes note-book, push with my heels, fit my knees into the desk, and spread the afternoon's work before me. I make policy notes about budget, property, and institutional management. An hour's research into the Mission's practices regarding size of allocations of capital funds from the Lottie Moon Christmas Offering gives me the handbook entry information I need. I type a stencil with the information to make copies for everyone and the board. Turning to correspondence I write two letters to the States and one to the local convention. With that completed and the papers in orderly stacks, I type a memo to members of the personnel committee of the Mission as a reminder for next week's meeting. With a final tap, I roll the last paper out of the typewriter and go for a cup of coffee before I start putting away the afternoon's efforts.

The front door opens and I hear David returning. He stops in the doorway.

"Charlie and I have been in the tree house."

"I can tell! You'd better get in the shower and give me that uniform to get back in shape for tonight."

The window chair invites me, and I slide into it with the cup to watch the roses grow a few minutes before hitting KP for supper preparation.

It would be easy to lie back in the thick of all this organization and let titles carry my contribution. No one is going to make me do anything. Well, except for the annual report and statistics that go to Richmond for the SBC Annual.

I tell the cup and the roses, "It would help if Latins were put together the way we are about reports, but they just don't do the numbers bit."

For several years, it has been my job to write the annual report, but I simply could not get all the data last year. The board cabled their reasonable request for my report. They had to get their reports in. But I had not been able to get complete statistics. I knew our unofficial increases, so I took the previous year's record and created the loveliest, most complete report I have ever sent from Paraguay. After I mailed it, I watched the sun a few days. It continued to rise in the east and set in the west.

As far as I know I am the only one who ever read it, but the act has given me great solace. When hard days have fallen, I've squared my shoulders and said, "Anybody who can make a creative contribution to the Southern Baptist Convention Annual can handle this!"

Grace to pardon from the responsibility would have been nice; but when it didn't come, I fell back on the law and decided the deed came under the category of having to get my ox out of the ditch on the sabbath. Of course, until there was transgression, there was no law.

I could let the titles carry my identity. I will not be forced to do anything. The board must have our record, but I, personally, don't have to send it. Somebody else will if I don't. Missionary life is the world's biggest honor system. The trap on the other side is to become compulsive and try to do all the minutiae of the jobs the title implies. I alternate between feelings of entrapment and security.

Standing, I hesitate in front of my shelves which hold my ministry symbols like a shrine. My eye trails past to the korn folder. Organization is designed to help with the work. When it doesn't, or if we need to catch our breath, the fun begins!

16
In Communication
with the Foreign Mission Board

Dr. Hoke Smith, Jr.
Field Representative
Buenos Aires, Argentina

DEAR HOKE,
Enclosed you will find minutes and a carbon of a letter to Dr. Means with the indicated matters for his attention.

We laborers in the kingdom up here in the hinterlands always appreciate your visits to our meetings with news of big city life in gaucho land. It is good to have the personal contact with the board that you always bring.

If you have questions or need my decoder ring for any of these materials, just send me a smoke signal!

CORDIALLY,
GLADYS

Dr. Frank K. Means
Secretary for Latin America
Richmond, Virginia

DEAR DR. MEANS,
Under separate cover I am sending you a copy of the Information and Procedure Manual. I believe we incorporated all your suggestions. We decided not to elaborate on the transfer of property title procedure since our Mission is still in the process of defining our local policy. Discussion in our group leans toward a procedure using the approved Brazilian system.

The part of the manual that is not yet approved is the section beginning on page 11, B. Capital Outlays, and running through the top part of page 16. This was sent "back to the drawing board" and I don't know how it will eventually evolve. It was not easy to get all the information in a systematized and easily-understood form. And it will be, doubtless, the most thoroughly-studied part of the booklet.

The Hobsons have arrived. They seem to feel right at home. Their eight-year-old son has formed a friendship with our little girls. He is David's age. Wilbur observed that this is the first time any of the Lewis women have had a tranquilizing effect on anyone.

I will send the final manual when it is ready.

SINCERELY,
GLADYS LEWIS

Mr. Cotton Wright
Business Manager
Richmond, Virginia

DEAR COTTON,
The papers with a breakdown and overage percentage for our baggage and the hospital freight have arrived with the charges to be made from our salary on a monthly quota for our portion.

I have done a thorough study of the inventories and barrel numbering sequence. If you will look on page 3 of the listing I sent you from our files and page 5 from the one from the freight company, you will find these to be for the hospital. My page 7 matches with the bottom half of page 2 and the top half of page 3 of the freight company. These two are also to be charged to the hospital.

In the customs fees, subtracting the proper percentage of overcharge for the above, which was not our property, will leave a total of $127.64, which we owe as our portion of the shipment.

THANK YOU VERY MUCH,
GLADYS LEWIS
PARAGUAY

Dr. Floyd North
Editor, *The Commission*
Richmond, Virginia

DEAR DR. NORTH,
Enclosed are two articles which may be in line with the kind of material we discussed.

I have discovered that people are enthralled by the kinds of things I do down here to keep a household running. My attempt is to tell our experience realistically, at least the way I perceive them. I want my writing to avoid moralizing about life here and, as well, any hint of longing for the USA. I thought a glimpse of how identification affects us would be inclusion of Karen's reaction to news of President Kennedy's death.

I said to her, "Karen, someone has killed our president."
She sucked in her breath, "What?"
"Someone has shot President Kennedy."
"Oh," she said in relief. "I thought you meant President Stroessner."

You will find that on page 4 near the bottom. If you think that would be misunderstood, feel free to remove it.

The other one shows how it is to be a citizen of two worlds and the love for both. I hope they show a little of the charm of the Paraguayan people.

A special insight into that grace for me is the account on page 7 of my taking visitors to the Government Palace downtown and one of the gardeners cutting a rose and asking me if he could have permission to make a presentation to my little girl. That may be too much for an American audience. If so, I have enough other illustrations without it.

Thank you for letting me write for *The Commission*. I love doing it.

SINCERELY,
GLADYS S. LEWIS
PARAGUAY

Mr. E. L. Deane
Treasurer
Richmond, Virginia

DEAR MR. DEANE,

Mr. Wright has written explaining the computation of freight charges and has indicated two or three errors I made in the submission of my record with that of the hospital shipment. I have his determination in hand.

He also defined your policy. I understand fully. The amount you mention as a salary deduction the next ten months will be acceptable.

YOURS TRULY,
MRS. WILBUR LEWIS
PARAGUAY

Edna Frances Dawkins
Personnel Department
Richmond, Virginia

DEAR EDNA FRANCES,

Loved your visit! I also loved the gift. I want to thank you for that unmentionable you brought me from the States. Such luxury!

Come back anytime. Wanda and I are always on Iguassu Falls call.

Viva Coca Cola!

LOVE,
GLADYS

Dr. Hoke Smith, Jr.
Field Representative
Buenos Aires, Argentina

DEAR HOKE,

You will find herein my usual pen pal stuff: handbook entries, minutes, and reports.

Wilbur and I loved having you for dinner while you were here.

I enjoyed the time you and I had to talk before Wilbur got home. The devotional messages you bring to the Mission are always watering-can fresh. I'm sure you have sensed another ministry you perform for all of us. In addition to being our fellow missionary, straw boss, and welcome visitor, there is a pastoral role you fill.

I have read and reread, with some of your comments as background, 1 and 2 Timothy, Galatians, and some of Philippians. I think sometimes I pray when I ought to be reading the Bible. I fall into thinking I know what God has said, and I'm not that certain he has heard what I said! I could be more deliberate about God's Word if I didn't have to make so many decisions on the hoof at a run about his world.

Come back anytime. You are one neat feller!

As Always,
Gladys

Mr. Louis Cobbs
Personnel Department
Richmond, Virginia

Dear Louis,

This is a note to tell you how much all of us enjoyed and appreciated your recent visit to Paraguay. You are, no doubt, fully recovered from the demands of travel and hard at work.

To show you just how much we enjoyed you, I am sending you a copy of the "minutes" from our meeting together. I hope you will get a coffee-break giggle or two from it. Only very special people are written up in these exclusive "minutes" that we keep!

Please give our regards to your co-workers.

Sincerely,
Gladys Lewis

Dr. Frank K. Means
Secretary for Latin America
Richmond, Virginia

Dear Dr. Means,

Enclosed is the composite report for the past year, a copy of the revised constitution of the Mission, and another little composition so you will know all the piety of the composite report did not ruin my pen. Actually, it was a bit of fun we had during a lull at the April meeting.

I still ponder over your exegesis of the first Psalm you gave us a couple of months ago when you were through here. My final line conclusion is not one you made, but I shall always think of you as that tree planted by the water. Your even-handed administration of all of us with fairness and tenderness is a warm and comforting experience for me. Your point was that the characteristics of the godly person in the first Psalm are worth imitating. My conclusion is that you are already there, treelike in the symbolism.

We enjoyed having the movie people here. My first venture into the world after the hepatitis bout was going to the market with Fon Scofield for some pictures Dr. North wanted for an article I have written. Leland Harper drove all of us down there. I felt rather ridiculous having four men help with the two baskets we took for the pictures when I usually haul out six or eight fully loaded. I told them they were ruining my reputation with the market women and causing me to lose face.

SIGNING OFF FROM DOWN SOUTH,
GLADYS

Genevieve Greer
Book Editor
Richmond, Virginia

DEAR MISS GREER,

I have received your letter with the information about the Christmas card activity in the teaching guide of my book.

It was good of you to check with the post office for mailing procedures to Paraguay for the children to use.

I do not mind at all being a "guinea pig" with this experiment. Glad to do it.

SINCERELY,
GLADYS LEWIS

Dr. Floyd North
Editor, *The Commission*
Richmond, Virginia

DEAR DR. NORTH,

I am sending you the enclosure entitled *Hoke*. We are in stunned shock and grief at his sudden death.

TRULY YOURS,
GLADYS S. LEWIS

Dr. Frank K. Means
Secretary for Latin America
Richmond, Virginia

DEAR DR. MEANS,

We have been writing you almost weekly about events here. There is no need to review and rehash them at this time. You have understood and been supportive of our anguish.

A time for definitive action has come and we have made a commitment to our sense of that reality.

On next Tuesday we will announce to the Mission our intention to return to the States to try to sort out our lives and our future.

We appreciate your counsel, spiritual advice, and listening ear. Our gratitude for you is surpassed only by our love.

At this moment we think we will be in Oklahoma within six weeks. We will be in touch here and will call you from there.

MOST SINCERELY,
WILBUR AND GLADYS LEWIS

17
In Culture Shock

The embassy secretary comes from the inner office. She is sleeveless and sandaled against the November heat. Pushing back her chair, she remains standing behind her desk.

"Mr. Reed says he can process your baby's birth certificate now if you'd like to wait. Or you may leave your papers and we'll have it for you tomorrow." Her professional courtesy almost covers her youth and inexperience.

There is no way I will let those papers out of my possession twenty-four hours, even if they are in the office at the American Embassy. "I'll wait," I smile.

"I noticed your little girl is seven weeks old. You are getting her birth registered quickly," she says in a Middle Western accent.

"She was born at the Baptist Hospital, so there was no problem with getting those papers. But I've spent a lot of time in the Paraguayan offices, getting the proper applications, stamps, and signatures."

"My apartment mate saw your husband a few months ago. She cut her hand on a broken glass."

"I hope it's all right now."

"She had twelve stitches in it. Scared me to death! She works in the ambassador's office. We had to double for her until she could use her hand."

"Did you work in the other wing?"

"I was in there the day a delegation from the State Department came through. I loved it!"

"When we first came to Paraguay, Prince Philip paid an official visit."

"Did you see him?"

"Certainly did. I took my children to the corner below the hospital where I knew the entourage would turn on Avenue Mariscal Lopez from the airport."

"Maybe you were on BBC!"

We laugh at the idea.

"General de Gaulle came too. We saw him twice."

"Where?"

"Same place as he came into town. When he left, my husband went with us and we drove to the airport."

"Could you get a good look at him?"

"He towered over everyone! We climbed up a flagpole stand and took pictures."

"Bet you make all the military parades."

"We've been to several. One time we got into a restricted area without realizing it. Our little boy has a toy clacker he started whirling. I thought the soldiers were going to shoot us before they realized we were harmless."

"I loved the Independence celebrations this year. This was a first for me since I have been here less than a year."

"The American Girl Scouts and I marched in the one last year. The presidential party in the reviewing stand saluted us! I thought it was because we were so sharp and smart, but later I remembered the ambassador's daughter is in my troop."

"Would you like a Coke?" she asks with a twinkle in her eye.

"Oh, please!"

"In a glass or bottle?"

"Bottle!" I can't believe my good fortune.

She is gone and back with a green bottle that carries a truckload of memory images of Oklahoma youth and US citizenship.

"Make yourself comfortable." She hands it to me and partially disappears behind the work on her desk.

I adjust my purse strap over my right shoulder and hold the

bottle with its precious contents like a priest lifts the host. Selecting a stuffed chair by a window that overlooks the immaculate embassy gardens, I sink into unexpected pleasure. My hands lock around the pale green transparent glass and caress the classic curves. I stare at the bottle mouth, into the transparent red-brown liquid, and savor the anticipated taste. Being an optimist by nature and a person of faith, I know that someday Paraguay will have Coca Cola. At the moment it does not.

A year ago, when Wanda Ponder and I took Edna Frances Dawkins, visiting from Richmond, to Brazil, we gathered all the Coke bottles in the Mission, three cases, for the express purpose of bootlegging a little bit of home back to our tribe. Whatever clothing or toiletries we carried had to fit in shoulder bags because hands had to be free for the heist.

Edna Frances was fresh from the US and our guest. We did not want to be less than gracious as hosts. But missionary morale was at stake. She had to carry a case too. Being from the board, she knew the importance of a steady missionary hand on the wheel of steerage for methods in missiology. Being at our post, we knew that hand was steadier if its right or left counterpart held a Coke!

At the time the road was not paved all the way, nor was there a bridge over the great Parana between Brazil and Paraguay. Leaving the Volkswagen on the Paraguayan side, we ferried across swirls and eddies with the empty bottles clutched to our hearts. Aside from the fact that the bottles cost more than the drink, we could not get the drink at all if we did not have bottles to leave in exchange for the ones we took.

Our purpose was to show Iguassu Falls to Edna Frances. It is a natural marvel of the world, over two miles wide, horseshoe-shaped and twice as high as Niagara, located between Argentina and Brazil, just over the Paraguayan border.

Being people of expedience as well as faith, we knew we had to find a trustworthy cache to leave our treasure until we could return to the town because of the amount of walking that faced us. Providence was good, and we found a shopkeeper who inspired our confidence.

On the return, the added weight of the liquid and the food we had eaten at the Old-World-style hotel at the falls pushed us mid-calf into the sand on the riverbanks as we labored to get down to the ferry. We sat huddled with Paraguayans and Brazilians in the vessel that putted across the whirling river with a water line only six inches below the edge of the boat. Calm and resignation were mine for I was prepared to meet capsizing and whirlpools with my case of Coca Cola wrapped in my arms.

I close my eyes and tilt the bottle to my mouth. Carbonated needles pummel my lips and shoot my nose. With the bottle down, I look at the surface bubbles on the drink, disappearing in the rupture from the medium that has held them in identity.

Looking about the room I see my president's picture and give him a nod and a thank-you wink for allowing overseas installations of the US Government to have Coca Cola. The Stars and Stripes hang on the wall beside him. I feel a familiar pride and lump in my throat and let my Coke-drinking ceremony take credit for tears in my eyes. The just-out-of-college-girl hovered at her work blesses me with the Americana she represents and has symbolically placed in my hands. I sip it and soak in the atmosphere of my native land.

I drink to one remaining swallow, then hold the bottle lightly by my side in the chair. A sheaf of leaflets on the table to my right catches my eye. I shuffle through them, select one captioned "Culture Shock," and lean back to scan it.

> Culture shock is the reaction experienced when confronted suddenly with living conditions, social customs, language, food, and geography radically different from those of one's customary or habitual lifestyle, presumably of one's national origin.

Could I embellish that for them!

Language school in Costa Rica was more of a prickle than a shock. There were adjustments to different housing and the schedule of going to school every day. No mistaking the switch from North American to Latin customs, but it was cushioned by adventure and the knowledge that it was only for a year.

The ocean voyage from New Orleans to Buenos Aires on a passenger liner was, in fact, a vacation dream.

But culture prickle advanced to jolt when we transferred in Buenos Aires to travel upriver nine hundred miles to Asuncion. Our home for the trip was a flat-bottomed riverboat that looked like the pictures of the old paddle wheelers that traveled the Mississippi.

Wilbur deposited the hand luggage, the children, and me in the place assigned to us and left to see to our baggage. I felt like a stranger in a strange land! Had I had a harp and a willow I would have hung the instrument on the tree and wept with God's children of that other Diaspora.

We were in a fairly large room on the first level in the bow of the boat. A porthole on either side gave light and sight outside. I looked out the one on the right and saw that it was broken. A few feet below me was the water line of the Parana. My eye trailed to the faded brocade curtain tied back from the porthole. Speckles of chewed orange pulp were stuck on it. I puzzled about how that could be and had just decided someone had missed the broken porthole while eating an orange and spitting the pulp, when the boat started with a lurch.

Only the fact that two small children clung to my skirts, the vague sensation that they were mine, and a remote memory of God having something to do with this, kept me from bolting.

I turned back to the porthole in the exact moment that the boat caught its first ocean swell since we were still in the mouth of the river, and the shooting wave splashed through the porthole to slap me full in the face. With choreographic precision, Wilbur opened the door at the moment of the assault, took in the scene, and turned on his heel to find us other quarters.

We were given a small stateroom on the third deck, but my gratitude swelled its proportions so that I did not notice stepping around and over stacked bags. Besides, I was too preoccupied with keeping two small children well back from the single rail on the walkway around the staterooms which was the only barrier between them and the river below.

We were traveling as first-class passengers. A charming doctor from Buenos Aires discovered Wilbur and tutored him in all things Latin and wonderful the entire trip. Only the last day while we waited in midriver to transboard a barge four hours below Asuncion did I interrupt and ask for help.

Latin people adore children. Blond, blue-eyed, two-year-old David was irresistible. While we waited for baggage to be loaded on the barge, I missed David. Frantically, I searched and found him by following the sound of his laughter. Men on the boat and men on the barge were playing with him by pitching him from boat to barge and back a distance of six feet with nothing to catch him but the river if they missed! Aggressive, cool, macho Wilbur put an end to it by saying apologetically, "His mother wants him."

I look at the Coke in my hand and think to myself, *Brushed my teeth with your Argentine sister on that trip.*

The water was not safe, so we drank bottled drinks and brushed our teeth with the same. Meals were a treat. We ate in a large dining room and were served course after course by waiters in white jackets. We picked up some manners too. One night we were brought apples on plates for the dessert course. I was on the verge of picking up mine to bite into it when a noise broke out that sounded like a sword fight between Attila the Hun and a Roman regiment. Lesson? Good etiquette dictates eating fruit with a knife and fork when served as dessert in Latin America.

Miss Americana switches on a desk fan, and I look up to see her putting weights on papers. I could have held down everything on that desk just with the heavy mood of my presence our first year, I think. It was probably the lowest point of my life.

Culture prickle and jolt turned to full shock when we achieved what we had spent so many years trying to attain—arrival.

First crack out of the box, I made a double contract on carrying our freight. When we touched the riverbank in the barge we had transboarded to, porters were all over us. Wilbur was at the front of the barge in a documents line, and I was widow-perched on our freight with the two little ones like a claim squatter. My first introduction to the *Guarani* language was a persistent porter who kept talking to me and waving a numbered metal disc with a chain on it in my face urging me to take it. I kept asking him to repeat what he was saying, all the while totally disillusioned because I had spent all those months learning Spanish and could not communicate one word with the first Paraguayan I met. He continued and gestured toward Wilbur.

"Did my husband send you?" Perfect Castilian.

"Si!" Perfect Castilian.

I let him thrust the coinlike object in my hand and watched baffled as he stood at attention beside me, assuming a palace guard stance in his faded khaki clothing. At length Wilbur reappeared with the hospital chauffeur who had found us. He had a numbered coin/chain and his own palace guard. Wilbur introduced us.

"This is Pastor Perez. He is from the hospital and has been watching for us since no one knew just when we would land."

"I am so pleased to meet you, *senora*. We are happy you are here."

His guard and my guard looked on with interest, smiling at the pleasant scene.

"We'll get your things off." He turned and began to give orders to his guard in Guarani. My guard stared in stunned disbelief. There broke out the biggest three-sided argument I have heard before or since. Not a word of it was understandable, but I could decipher from the looks and the gestures that I was the center of the problem. Finally, Pastor switched to Spanish and said to Wilbur,

"Doctor, may I speak privately with you?"

I watched the four of them go a few steps to the right. Pastor placed his hand on Wilbur's elbow. I could not hear, but the facial expressions and solemn nodding of his head told me the seriousness of the conversation. Tiring of all that, I began to look about. Paraguay was about me. I wanted to see it.

At length Wilbur returned and asked for the coin/chain I was swinging in my hand.

"What's wrong?"

"You made a labor contract with that porter."

"Didn't you send him to me?"

"I never laid eyes on him until I saw him with you."

The man would not take back his coin/chain, and we eventually paid him the price of his "contract" to get him to take it back and not take us to labor court.

Culture shock hit me like electric shock treatments. I hated the heat, the dirt, the smells. Essential chores took so much energy that there was no strength left for creativity or introspection to recharge batteries.

The missionaries seemed delighted to have us, as did the nationals. But our missionary and national brothers and sisters were only a handful in the total scene that was Paraguay.

We were unnoticed mainly. I would spend the major part of a day getting food for my household, or whatever was the living chore assignment for the day. Near the end of the searches and stops, I would feel an urge to stop a Paraguayan on the street and ask, "Does it matter to you that I have spent ten years of my life preparing to come here to help you and I spend my days buying cheese or flour or standing in lines to get permission to go stand in another line?"

The knowledge that the answer would be *no* kept me from asking. But the same knowledge helped me to learn that in many respects I had to learn to be my own support system. I needed triple ego strength. I had to make my decisions, act upon them, and stand by them after I had acted. Part of the depression that settled about me was sadness and anger from impatience to know our future and what was going to happen to us. I wanted shortcuts through all I had to learn to arrive at assimilation into the life and experience of another people.

I trace Coca Cola on the bottle with the corner of the leaflet. Culture shock! The things I tried!

Some inner grace always kept me aware that the problem was with me, not Paraguay. That was harder to handle. For I would tell myself all the reasons why I should not feel the way I did and then feel worse for still feeling that way. I was like someone on a life support system going out to be a rescuer.

At the deepest point in the pit, I hit on a very practical scheme. In desperation one day, I decided I would write down all the things I didn't like. Line followed line. Nothing was too insignificant.

Then I made another list of what I liked, for there were several by then, and determined to add another item each day.

After a while I felt a relaxation of tension and excitement about the positive list. Periodically I checked the black (bad) list and found those things less troublesome. The blue (good) list continued to grow. Into the process of the "black and blue" lists, my sense of humor began to return. With the outlet of the ukulele and my silly songs, I was on my way.

In a few months, I needed neither list for support. By then I had become acquainted with people and had identification with a group. Paraguayans are warm and gracious. We liked each other and then we loved each other. When I loved Paraguayans, I loved Paraguay. Love is collective only in its results. At its inception it is individual, one to one, or it is not love. Only after it is one to one can it go from one to group and from group to one.

I turn the bottle and swirl the last swallow. I'm told I'll have culture shock in reverse when I return to the States. I already dreaded the hurry, the impatience, the indifference.

Good and bad are in both places. One good is not better than another good, nor is one bad worse than another bad. We accept that both exist in both places and work with the realities of either sphere when we are present in it.

A buzzer sounds on Miss Americana's desk. She rises and goes to the inner office. Returning, she hands me a manila envelope with the seal of the US Government on it.

"Your papers and the birth certificate are inside."

"Thank you." I take them and look at my Coke. "I appreciate this too."

She leans toward me and whispers, "Take the bottle."

"But it's expensive. You can't get the bottles here."

"It's a baby gift from me to your baby's mother!"

In the car I drain the last drop of the last swallow, then roll the culture shock leaflet and stick it in the mouth of the bottle to soak any moisture.

"Don't want to shock you with a Coca Cola spill," I say to the American eagle protecting my baby's birth certificate. "I'm such a person of culture."

18
In Resignation

"Wait here. I'll get our tickets."

Each of our children stands guard by his or her assigned bags at the lake port in La Paz, Bolivia. With eyes puffy from crying and lack of sleep, I watch Wilbur stride to the window to buy our passage on the hydrofoil that will take us across Lake Titicaca from the Bolivian side to Corcovado on the Peruvian side. Taxis will be waiting for us to drive all afternoon around the northwestern part of the shoreline to Puno. We have train reservations in Puno to go across the Andes to Cuzco, ancient capital of the Incas, and Machupicchu, their lost sacred city. From Lima, the trip continues through Panama to Acapulco, Houston, and Oklahoma City. We have a two-week pilgrimage mapped out, before going home, to say good-bye to South America. It will put some time, as well as space, between us and the events of the past year. Those happenings have hammered us to a pulp the past four months.

I look at the sturdy little Lewis baggage sentinels. They are sharing candy from the box Karen dropped out the hotel window in town. It fell five floors and none spilled. They are avoiding any possible loss.

How many times have we carried them around this continent with the code? Each is responsible to watch two bags and the child next youngest, with the authority line running to the oldest one present. To have something to do, I fill my numb mind with names of countries where we have traveled—Costa Rica, Guatemala, Nicaragua, Chile, Brazil, Argentina, Bolivia, Peru.

The bags contain everything we own except for the small crate we shipped last week. Everything was sold except the silver, our pictures, a round leather table, the marble-based table mirror, an upright Steinway piano, and my harp.

I was glad when we decided we could take the piano. It was my pride. I enjoyed it because of the Kintners, our special friends from the Disciples Mission. I wanted it the first time I saw it, before it was mine. They left Paraguay six years ago. They were to go after her baby came. Each time she was in for a prenatal check Wilbur forgot to ask about the piano. While she was on the table, about to deliver, he turned to Bob and said, "By the way, Gladys wants to buy your piano."

From the table came Sallie's weak, "Tell him yes!" Having it will give me some continuity with the trauma of selling nearly all I owned.

Wilbur is inching closer to the window in the line. The children look about with unmasked curiosity. By habit I check off the number of bags with an experienced eye. We're crazy to go through South and Central America by plane, boat, and train with four children and all those bags. We should have sold it all!

Three weeks ago I put price tags on our possessions and set them in the yard for friends and strangers to examine. They went fast. Some disappeared too fast!

The third day of the sale I turned at Nilda's tugging. She and a neighbor were pointing at a man and a girl walking out the gate.

"They stole some of your clothes, *senora*."

The next day the couple returned. The girl had an inch of white tricot Sears half-slip hanging below the hem of her dress.

"You have on my slip."

"No, *senora*. This is mine."

I took her by the hand and led her to a corner of the house, pulled up her dress, and pulled down my slip.

"Step out of it."

She did.

"Leave."

She did.

Wanda and Gilda, walking up the driveway, witnessed the show. I answered the question in Wanda's eyes before she could speak.

"She stole my slip. I would have given it to her if she had asked."

"Mother, I'm thirsty," Karen says. "Is it too soon to have a drink?"

"Take just a sip. The water has to last until we get to the hotel tonight."

She takes the bottle of water with her name on it from her woven travel bag and touches it to her mouth. The action triggers parched throats from her siblings and a ritual of bottle searches and tongue wettings ensues.

I look from the shelter where we wait toward the lake and watch two Quechua Indians at work on their reed boats with high Viking-looking prows. They have on brightly colored skullcaps with long ear pieces that come well over their ears and turn up, protecting them from the cold. Their faces have the adenoidal look that results from centuries of ancestors breathing the high, thin Andean air with open mouths in order to get every bit of oxygen available. A shawl-wrapped woman saunters among us, wearing a black bowler hat and casually offering her wares from a basket of bread-looking food.

To the east the city with its look of modernity rises above the brown moonscape of this high plateau. It is lovely and interesting, but two days are enough. I'm in so much emotional pain I couldn't appreciate the Taj Mahal right now. My thoughts return, as metal shavings to a magnet, to the Asuncion airport two nights ago.

Our church people from Fernando and Sajonia were there; the household members we left, Nilda, Irma, and Catalino; and the hospital employees. One of the most loving gestures of this nightmare was the petition they all signed and brought to the house. In beautiful, flowing Spanish, they said they wanted us to stay with them, that they didn't care if Wilbur couldn't practice medicine, that together we'd find something in God's will he could do. With great effort, I composed a letter of gratitude and tried tenderly to explain that we did not feel the Lord would guide us through all that had been necessary for Wilbur to be a surgeon and then not intend for it to be used. Our missionary brothers and sisters were there: the Hickmans, Nicholses, McDowells, Skinners, Watsons, and Watkinses, I clung to each and felt my heart sliced away strip by strip.

The memory of words and embraces blurs with my tears. On the plane to La Paz I thought I would surely die from pain and felt as though the skin had been peeled from my body. I sat raw and bleeding.

Two days in La Paz have given me a thin crusting over the rawness, but every thought or memory jangles the hurt.

"Anybody try to pick you up?" Wilbur is in front of me with long strings of tickets.

I smile him an *A* for effort. "Chivalry is not dead."

"Is that yes or no?"

"No man looks at a woman with four kids."

"I do."

"You're handicapped. You're married."

He pats my elbow. "Saddle up, gang. We're set for Peru."

A boy steps in front of us. "*Senor*, my friend and I will carry your bags to the boat."

"How much?" He winks at me over their heads.

"Very cheap."

"OK. Get your shoulder bags, kids. We'll bring the rest."

Karen takes David's hand and Leanne's. I pick up Cristen. We walk leaning backward down a steep incline, then scramble over a bumpy gangway to the hydrofoil that will skim over the water to Corcovado and the taxis. We find window places and settle ourselves. The boys stack the bags around us, Wilbur pays them and then climbs in beside us. From their bows and the looks on their faces, I guess he emptied our remaining Bolivian money in their hands.

"Daddy, I don't have any place to put my coloring book."

"A nice man is going to talk to us, Leanne. He's going to tell us about the lake and the people who used to live here."

"When can I color?"

"We'll be on the boat a long time."

The boat fills with passengers and then begins to move on the lake. A brown-uniformed man picks up a mike and flips a switch that lights a map on the wall behind him.

"Is that where we are?" Karen asks.

"We are at the lower part. Titicaca is the name of the lake we are on and the Andes Mountains of Bolivia are on the south and east. Peru, where we are going, is on the west and north."

The brass square on the front of the man's hat has a number I can't determine from here. He has the lovely olive skin of Latin America, a bristly black mustache, crinkled black hair under his hat, and tinted glasses. He does not have the adenoidal look of the highlands.

"*Buenos dias*, ladies and gentlemen."

I fall under the spell of Latin charm and language. He begins a lecture about the area. As the boat turns and speeds on its air cushion, he begins a legend of beginnings that has similarities with our creation narrative in Genesis.

"In the beginning . . ."

In the beginning, ten years ago, we knew we faced difficulties in getting a license to practice medicine in Paraguay. Franklin Fowler, Bill Skinner, and Don McDowell before us had faced the struggle, but eventually came out with permanent licenses. We knew the road they had traveled: the dual relationship with the Health Ministry, that grants permission to practice, and the medical school, that offers the examinations leading to authentication and approval to receive a license.

In Oklahoma medical schools provide the education and the State Board of Medical Examiners gives the testing and legal recognition. Once education is completed, licensure occurs within a couple of days upon passing the state board exams and a physician is duly licensed to practice.

Paraguay's educational system is patterned after the European model. The university is a strong, autonomous unit with little control or intervention from the government. The liberal arts foundation comes through the high school and students go directly into their professional school at the university. They bypass a liberal arts undergraduate program, but spend six years in medical school. The different schools, or *facultades,* become very strong entities within the university system. There is neither reciprocity or state board. A person desiring a license must obtain one the way everyone else does, by taking and passing all the oral exams of each of the six years of medical school. Our three predecessors, with varying degrees of ease and difficulty, had gotten through the exam process by petitioning and convening the professors, usually three, who gave each exam.

Wilbur came prepared to do the same. He had notarized copies of his university and medical school work, state board, and Oklahoma license. At first he took his documents to the medical school and then to the ministry with a note that he was seeking authorization to take the exams leading to a permanent license. The vice-minister gave him a permission to practice, with periodic renewal as long as he was in the exam process. Wilbur then returned the papers to the university to be accepted and to be granted the formal approval to proceed with testing.

But we had come in a different time. Nationalism was stronger. There were political in-house factors that did not pertain to us, but to which we fell prey and pawn. The papers were held up for months in the office of the dean of the law school, who had the prerogative of determining their validity.

At last, with counsel from our missionary colleagues and others, an audience was sought with the rector of the university, a friend to our hospital and work. With his intervention, the papers moved on to the medical school. Resistance was met in convening an examining counsel, but finally a date was set for three Paraguayan doctors to give Wilbur an oral anatomy exam. After lengthy Spanish questions, the three gave their decision. Wilbur Lewis, graduate of a class A US medical school, licensed physician of the state of Oklahoma, recipient of intern and surgical residency training in the finest hospitals in the Southwestern United States, had failed anatomy.

"The conquistadores came to this area in the 1500s looking for gold and silver."

Maybe we can trace it to them. Perhaps it was a deep-seated hatred of anything that goes back to colonialism or smacks of foreign control.

It helped later to learn from one of our Paraguayan doctor friends that the principal examiner had boasted ahead of time that he was not going to pass Wilbur.

"I'm going to ask him things he's never heard of, and if he can answer, I still am going to fail him," our friend reported the words of the anatomy professor.

Then rules began to change. Wilbur returned to the medical school to petition for another exam.

"We no longer call special examinations. You must take them when the medical students take them."

"When is that? Where may I get a list of all that is offered?"

"You do not understand. You must start at the beginning and take just the exams of that year at that class level. You will progress a year at a time."

"How many times a year do the students take exams?"

"Two, maybe three times."

We settled into that routine. There was no problem as far as medical practice was concerned for the permission from the ministry was valid as long as he continued in the process. Wilbur dutifully went to classes prior to test time to meet new professors and sat for oral exams with the students—"his class."

I lean my head on Wilbur's shoulder and chuckle over a memory of "his class."

"That's a welcome sound," Wilbur says.
"Mee-stair Park-air!" I exaggerate.
We both laugh at the inside joke.

Pluma in Spanish means feather. It also means pen. An idiomatic expression uses *pluma* to describe an elegant looking person. The Parker pen is imported and well known as a US product. Because Wilbur always wore a suit and tie, the students nicknamed him Mister Parker, the sartorial *gringo pluma,* in the inverted humor of youth and offer of affection.

We were slowed by student strikes, but Wilbur was never failed again. In fact, some of the professors were friendly, even embarrassed by his treatment. Prior to the time he was to retake the anatomy exam, the principal examiner who had caused the problem earlier, showed up at the hospital one day. Quite jovially the man said he'd be pleased to see him again, and by the way, did Wilbur have access to automobile parts from the US? He had a Nash Ambassador with a broken taillight cover and he could not get the parts in Asuncion.

Wilbur sent an emergency message to my brother-in-law.

"Send a Nash Ambassador taillight cover. Send two. If in doubt, send the whole car."

The shipment arrived before the exam time and was delivered. The test was a piece of cake!

Before we went on furlough, Wilbur called on the vice-minister to tell him we were going to the States and that the permit would expire while we were away.

"I want to tell you I will be back, and I will request renewal at that time," he said.

Upon returning, we discovered the man had died of a heart

attack while we were gone. Wilbur called on the new vice-minister, showed him the letters of permission from the previous official, told him of his visit prior to leaving and of the verbal agreement they had. Authorization was granted for another conditional license under the terms of the previous one, and we went on as before.

A year ago, as Wilbur was beginning his fifth year at the medical school, a new minister of health was appointed by the president.

Cristen's head nods one final release into sleep.

"Let's put her on this seat and move up by Leanne," I suggest to Wilbur.

"Mommie, the man's going to talk all day! I want to draw!" Leanne complains.

"Where's your paper?" I ask.

She shuffles things in her bag and brings out a tablet and pencil.

"Help me make the outline."

"What do you want to draw?"

"Daddy's hospital!"

I sketch an outline I hope she'll accept.

"I'll put in the windows! Here's Uncle Leland's office and where Mario works and the big meeting room and . . ."

The big meeting room. The big meeting.

Within days the new minister's office notified the hospital that an inspection would be made in September. The situation was so mysterious that we asked our lawyer to be present. Bill Skinner also invited the American consul to be present. There was an ugly fear of possible nationalization of our property.

A month later a report came saying all was satisfactory except that someone was practicing medicine in the hospital without a license.

We then procured the services of a lawyer in the dominant political party and began attempts to have an audience with the minister. The point was to clarify the wording of the October communication which said Wilbur's status had never been legal.

A strategy in Latin American politics in nullifying an opponent is the negating of the predecessor's decisions by the one who comes to power. The man who had granted the permit was out of favor, therefore, all he had done was illegal! A pawn, again.

In our audience with the minister, we wanted to ask him to revoke the license instead of declaring that it was illegal. The standing language, in effect, ruled the work of nine years to be invalid.

A date was given for the interview. The missionaries assigned to the hospital and some Paraguayan physicians formed the cadre that accompanied Wilbur.

I paced the floor at home and waited.

"What?" I turn at the tug on my arm.

"I said I'm surprised that my history buff is not writing this down. He's talking about how the Incas outsmarted the Spaniards," Wilbur says.

"I'm listening."

"The Incas moved their treasure from place to place and would tell the Spaniards where it was, but by the time the conquerors arrived, the treasure was gone to another place."

I stare at our guide and his face turns to Wilbur's above despondent shoulders as he walked in the front door the day of the meeting.

"What happened? What did he say?" I asked.

He kicked off his shoes and flopped in a chair. "He said he wants to help us and clarify my position."

I caught my breath. "He did? That's wonderful!"

"He told us four ways he could help us with my situation. One, if we would supply an office in the hospital for someone from his office to register births. Easy to see that. With our small birth number in comparison with other facilities and all the midwives, that would be a ruse to have an information link to his office to keep us at a disadvantage. Then, he said he knew our good charity work and that we were interested in helping people. Because he is in a better position to know the people to be helped he wanted us to authorize him to admit charity patients."

"It wouldn't work, would it?"

He punched a pillow with his fist. "He'd load us up with political debts! First time we crossed one, the ministry would be howling at us! You'll love the next one. He said he knew the work of the mobile clinic and he wants to help us with it. Wants one of his people from the ministry to go with us to help with facilities and prevent problems."

"They'd put us at the political party headquarters in each town! It would cut away our identity with the churches!" I gasp.

"That's the picture."

"The hospital, the Convention, the Mission won't agree to it, will they?"

"I won't agree to it! They won't use me to get at our work!"

"You said four things."

"Said he knew we wanted to have the best medical staff in the country and that we worked with Paraguayan physicians. He wants authority to select those to be on our staff. He said he knew the political party of all on our staff and too many of them are members of opposing parties."

"I don't even know the parties of our doctors."

"Two are in other parties. The rest are either members of the minister's party or are nothing," stated Wilbur.

"Two out of all our doctors are too many?"

"Apparently. We'll have to deny that one too. Religious and moral values take precedence over political alliance."

"Have you already formed a reply?"

"We talked on the way home. This will have to be drafted with our lawyer."

With the reply formed, Wilbur presented it through his liaison at the ministry. In conversation, he learned the nursing school and the charity pharmacy were also under attack.

In January, a specialist who is on our consulting staff, and works at the ministry as well, called Bill to tell him a surprise investigating team was on their way to the hospital. Wilbur had not practiced medicine since the confusion began in October but was doing hospital administration while Leland was on furlough. He was in the hospital but went home when told of the impending visit.

Two official-looking men came to the appointment desk and asked to be seen as patients by Dr. Lewis.

The receptionist said, "Dr. Lewis is not taking care of patients now and hasn't since October."

"That concludes this segment of the lecture. We'll have another when we stop for awhile at Moon Island." Our guide snaps off his lights and places the pointer behind the lectern.

"I'm hungry, Mother."

"You always are, Bodge." I ruffle his hair. "We could all use a snack." I pass crackers, cheese, and hard candy from my bag.

"This tastes like the candy at Camboriu," Karen says.

"The beach was not as crowded there this year," says Wilbur as he selects a piece of candy.

"February was later in the season than we've gone before," I explain.

"I didn't have a lull in my hospital problems earlier."

"Was good to leave them."

"The Swiss feel of the hills around Camboriu were just what I needed," Wilbur says.

"The Tiroliza was my luxury," I say. "Can't think of anything better than a full breakfast laid on checkered linen after thirty extra minutes of sleep each day."

"I'll never forget the moon and the beach the night we walked it so late. That's when I knew we couldn't stay in Paraguay." He stares across the water.

"Coming home to the minister's signed decree left no doubt," I say quietly.

"'Wilbur Lewis cannot practice medicine until his exams are

completed and will limit his duties to hospital administration.' He not only told me what I couldn't do, but what I had to do."

"Mommie, will the other people give Duchess crackers?" Cristen asks.

"I told them she likes crackers."

"She'll be scared in their backyard."

"They love her as we do. They'll take care of her, and she'll get used to a new place to live."

"Can we get another swing when we get to Oklahoma?"

"We'll see."

"Just like our swing we left?"

"There will never be another like the swing we left."

A dozen ideas came and went in my attempt to take the swing. I decided to throw myself on Wilbur's generosity, try to tell him the swing's importance. If my survival depended on it, he'd find a way to ship it. In the end I just said, "Do you suppose we could dissemble the swing some way and take it with us?"

"I don't see how. It's so big and heavy that shipping would cost a fortune." He lifted a box of things to take to the hospital and carried them with a pregnant walk down the hall. I stared long and hard through the window at my holy of holies maintaining its silent sacredness in my temple yard. Tree movement from the avocado and pine beyond alerted me to life and growth in my temple court woods. Altars are needed, but life is better. I began the slow process of transferring the swing inside my heart court.

The night we decided to tell the Mission we were leaving we sat together in the swing, sharing each other's pain.

Wilbur said with gentleness and tenderness, "I think we must leave. Can you come to that belief?"

The moon was on duty on the opposite side of the world, collecting sun to reflect. My sky was dark. I looked up at the black velvet night pinned in place by diamond chip stars, and the beauty and preciousness of it almost choked all breath away. The Christmas Tree and the Southern Cross seemed closer than I remembered, almost as though they'd moved that way to be able to send me more warmth.

The Foreign Mission Board had been apprised all along of the developments. So we wrote the letter saying we were leaving. We both signed it and went in the car into Asuncion in the middle of the night to mail it. We didn't talk. In my irrationality, I expected some form of deliverance at every corner. When it didn't come, I felt something would happen at the post office. We both put the letter in the slot, but the only thing that happened was the letter made a little click when it hit the bottom.

"Do you suppose Jim Howell thinks we're crazy?" I ask, wondering about our personal lawyer's reaction to all that had happened to us.

"He has kept all my other papers in his Midwest City office. I told him when I certified copies of all my documents here and sent them to him that there was probably no cause to do what I was doing. I didn't want to be caught in some legal tangle here without proof."

"You sent him a copy of everything that happened?"

"Every paper."

"Anything about seeking the audience with the president?"

"I sent the papers before we decided to go to the palace. Remember how we talked about it for weeks, wondering if we should."

"It was risky."

"Our lawyer here couldn't be sure if the minister were acting on his own or on orders."

"So much happened so fast."

"That good-bye to us in the Villa Morra church bulletin started the whirl."

"Georgina." I smile. "Do you suppose she learned her ability to order things from her husband and moving in military circles all her life?"

"The bulletin sent her to the president's barber."

"That's almost an Esther story."

"She used those words to him." We sit thinking of the devout, humble man in another church, personal barber to the president.

I ask, "Do you think the president really does consider him his spiritual adviser?"

"I've heard it said several times."

"What do you suppose he thought of Georgina saying God had given him that position to save the Baptist Hospital?"

"She told him what to say when the president called for a haircut and listed several facts, one after another, for him to tell."

"I never believed the president had a part in causing any of the problems," I looked out on water stretching as far as we can see.

"The president knows us and our work. I operated on the wife of his chauffeur."

"I never knew that!"

"Just because I'm in trouble doesn't mean I don't have connections," Wilbur grins.

"Big Tuesday."

"Bill and I had spent the afternoon with the lawyer making our strategy for an audience on Friday."

"The hospital people thought our troubles were over because the barber had been called and had told the president." I trace my fingernail on the seat cushion.

"Things had gotten too complex."

"Wish I could have seen the minister's face when the president called him!" I jab a seat cushion button with my forefinger.

"I've recreated that scene, the president standing, going to the phone, calling the minister. I especially enjoy his shouting three times that the minister should help us," Wilbur recalls.

"*Ayudales* ('help them')! Three great yells."

"I knew it was too late for me."

"It did solve things for the nursing school and the hospital."

"But I had that decree signed by the minister. The lawyer thought we could make him rescind it, knowing what we knew; but some officials would resign to save face rather than take back a decree. If he did take it back, he would be so mad at me personally and the hospital, he would forever look for ways to get even.

Karen says, "I'm sorry I left Paraguay without knowing the president's barber."

David asks, "Why? You don't know President Nixon's barber."

"He hasn't helped us!" She gives her brother a hopeless look.

"I felt my removal would allow everyone on both sides to restore rapport between the hospital and the ministry. They need each other."

"We need them! They need us!" I exclaim.

He clasps an arm about my shoulders. "They don't need us. They'll be fine. We'll take our treasure and move on."

"What treasure?"

"Our calling."

The guide walks to his mike and points out Moon Island to us. "We will be disembarking in ten minutes for a visit." He goes on to tell and Incan legend of the fleeing Indians who dumped their treasure in the bottomless Titicaca between Moon and Sun Islands rather than surrender it to the Spaniards.

I brood over the inverted parable between the Spaniards and the Incas and us and the ministry. The lake has enough treasure. We won't leave ours.

The raw places ease a bit. I feel the growth of new skin.

Epilogue:
In a Call to Mission

Here I sit, looking at this manuscript which details another life, years removed from the events, but close as breath to the memory of them.

What do you do when you feel like your call is recalled?

You continue in faith, watching skin a bit scarred replace itself, until you finally understand that calling is commitment, not geography. It can be renounced, but is never revoked.

Now I live and work in a different area of Christian missions, but my call to commitment is unchanged from the days when I served in Paraguay.

After we had been gone from Paraguay four years, we returned for a visit. The medical and church work had gone on without us. It was thriving, in fact. Yet, our mark was in it. There is a sense in which we are all replaced, as well as a sense in which no one can be replaced.

When the hospital celebrated its twenty-fifth anniversary, we were sent copies of the ceremonies. The minister who had caused our problems was a program personality. My anger tossed the paper in the fire. Quick insight snatched it back and saved it. His presence sealed the acceptance of our sacrifice.

Part of Yahweh's atonement acts in the holy of holies involved the scapegoat for ancient Israel's woes.

The day the program came, I grew one square foot of new skin, and the pet goats, Wilbur and Gladys, skipped on into the wilderness.

I planted sixteen trees in my yard in Asuncion. There were no cottonwoods, but I had the swing; and I wept when I left it. I cannot find one here like it, and no one will repeat my design.

Many cottonwoods are mine now. They line the creek that moats my house. Upstairs is a writing cubicle, my own embryonic sac where I recreate myself by pouring me through ink onto paper, a wood product as the swing was.

The recreation is a creation that renews me.

I do not understand the process, but I know the creation connects with other altars in other minds.

The cottonwoods and my cubicle have replaced the swing, my veiless holy of holies.

Of the lessons from Paraguay, the one that empowers me day by day is the mandate to live in the present, in and by the Presence.

I've had enough of present living now to cushion the pain of that lost past.

I have skin again—scarred in places, grafted in others, and some fresh as a baby's. But it is all new and vital. I can recall that past, and the agony once known in its passing is balanced by the joy of the passage.

I want to share my earth as it *was* On Earth as It *Is*.

And if I ever find the swing and it is made of cottonwood, I will sell my kingdom to buy it, for that will be heaven for me On Earth as It Is.